THE GREAT MYST

A DAVID & CHARLES BOOK

David & Charles is an F+W
Publications Inc. company
4700 East Galbraith Road
Cincinnati, OH 45236

First published in the UK in
2007

© 2007 E-ducation.it, Firenze
A SCALA Group company
www.e-ducation.it
info@e-ducation.it

This 2007 edition published
by David and Charles by
arrangement with E-ducation.it.

Project Director: Cinzia Caiazzo
Editor-in-chief: Filippo Melli
Texts: Tatiana Pedrazzi
Editorial Staff: Giulia
Marrucchi, Sibilla Pierallini
Captions: Francesca Taddei
Graphics: Maria Serena Di
Battista
Translation: Heather Mackay
Robert

Photographs:
© 2007 Archivio Fotografico
SCALA GROUP
© SCALAGROUP and COREL
All rights reserved
© Lange/Fondazione Archivio
Lange
© Archivi Alinari, Firenze:
© Robert Rive/Museo di Storia
della Fotografia Fratelli Alinari,
© Bridgeman Art Library/Alinari

© De Agostini: © W. Buss/De
Agostini, © Foglia/De Agostini,
© G. Veggi/De Agostini
© Giovanni Caselli

Illustrations, selected from the
Scala Archives, of property
belonging to the Italian
Republic are published by
concession of the competent
authority (Ministero per i Beni
e le Attività Culturali).

A catalogue record for this
book is available from the
British Library.

ISBN-13: 978-0-7153-2764-7
paperback
ISBN-10: 0-7153-2764-X
paperback

Printed in China
for David & Charles
Brunel House   Newton
Abbot   Devon

Visit our website at www.
davidandcharles.co.uk

David & Charles books
are available from all good
bookshops; alternatively you
can contact our Orderline on
0870 9908222 or write to
us at FREEPOST EX2 110,
D&C Direct, Newton Abbot,
TQ12 4ZZ (no stamp required
UK only); US customers call
800-289-0963 and Canadian
customers call 800-840-5220.

THE GREAT MYSTERIES OF ARCHAEOLOGY

POMPEII

D&C
David and Charles

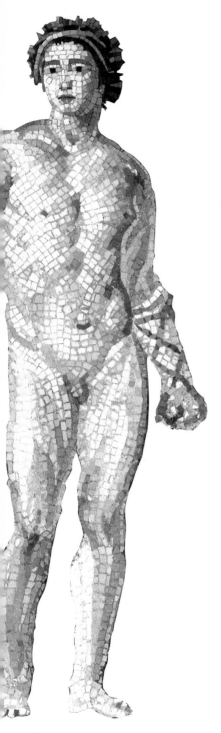

TABLE OF CONTENTS

CHAPTER 1

9 **THE DISCOVERY**

10 THE DISCOVERY OF POMPEII

12 THE DISCOVERY OF HERCULANEUM

16 JOHANN JOACHIM WINCKELMANN

18 Travellers and Artists

20 The Pompeian Style

22 THE FIRST SCIENTIFIC EXCAVATIONS

28 DISCOVERIES IN THE 20TH CENTURY

34 THE MYSTERIES OF POMPEII: DIONYSIAN RITUAL IN THE VILLA OF THE MYSTERIES

CHAPTER 2

45 **THE REMAINS OF A CIVILIZATION**
POMPEI: DAILY LIFE

46 THE ORIGINS OF POMPEII

50 The Etruscans at Pompeii

52 The Greek Influence

54 From Samnite to Roman Domination

60 THE BIRTH OF THE ROMAN COLONY

62 The Beginning of the Imperial Age

66 A Violent Earthquake

67 The Emperor Titus: a Troubled Reign

68 The City Buried by Vesuvius

70 URBAN DEVELOPMENT

74 Private Houses: Spatial Arrangement

78 Large Public Buildings

82 Entertainment: the Amphiteatre and the Theatre

88 The Baths

90 ART: WALL PAINTING

95 The Mosaics

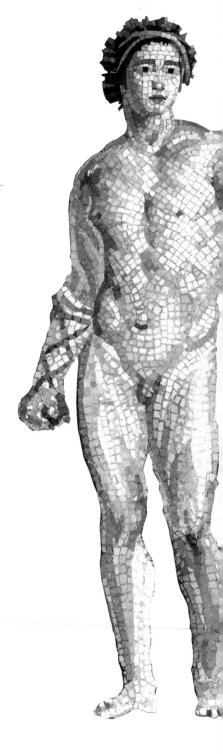

100 **SCULPTURE**

102 **ECONOMIC LIFE:
AGRICULTURE
AND LIVESTOCK**

108 Oil and Wine: from
Production to Sale and
Consumption

113 Slaves

116 Arts and Crafts

123 Flourishing Commercial
Activity

126 **DAILY LIFE**

130 The Banquet: a Social
Festivity

135 Medicine and Health

138 The Role of Women in
Marriage and the Family

142 Fashion, Dress and
Make-up

146 School and Education

149 Popular Entertainment:
Games and Spectacles

160 **RELIGIOUS LIFE:
THE ROMAN PANTHEON**

163 The Capitoline Trinity

164 Pompeii: a City
Dedicated to Venus

168 The Cult of Apollo

170 Mystery Cults and
Oriental Divinities

172 The Iseum at Pompeii

CHAPTER 3

175 **THE SITE TODAY**

176 **RESTORATIONS
AT POMPEII**

178 **THE NATIONAL
ARCHAEOLOGICAL
MUSEUM IN NAPLES**

180 **EXHIBITIONS ON POMPEII**

181 **THE AREA
SURROUNDING POMPEII**

182 **HERCULANEUM**

188 **THE VILLAS
AT BOSCOREALE
AND OPLONTIS**

189 Visiting Pompeii Today

Garden with stone heads of Hermes and a fountain, Pompeii. This wall painting from the House of the Golden Bracelet bears witness to the highly civilized life enjoyed in the city.

THE DISCOVERY

Spectacular image of a volcanic eruption. A similar eruption by Vesuvius in 79 AD destroyed Pompeii.

On 24 August in 79 AD Vesuvius unexpectedly erupted after lying dormant for hundreds of years. With incredible speed a thick coat of hot ash and pumice covered the densely populated area at the foot of the volcano. The city of Pompeii was totally buried and most of its inhabitants killed: their lives stilled forever as they were caught by a lethal torrent of volcanic gas and rock fragments when disaster struck. The rapid and complete burial of the city, with the loss of all its monuments and every sign of human life, was followed by long centuries of oblivion before Pompeii was discovered, by chance, almost intact. But it was not until the 16th century that the architect Domenico Fontana stumbled on some inscriptions and the remains of a building while working on a development project in the valley of the Sarno. At first nobody associated his finds with the ancient and almost forgotten city of Pompeii, although his discovery aroused the interest of collectors and treasure seekers.

THE DISCOVERY OF POMPEII

Pierre Jacques
Volaire, *Eruption
of Vesuvius,*
Hermitage
Museum,
St Petersburg.

Towards the mid-18th century
the first excavations were
undertaken at Pompeii under
the Bourbon king Charles III
of Naples. In 1757 the house
of Jiulia Felix was discovered,
while the first inscription
bearing the name of the
city was dug up in 1763.

Efforts then became more
concentrated but followed
no scientific method: the

unauthorised removal of statues and other remains was a constant problem. A royal decree designed to put a halt to these depredations had little effect. The ruling family's enthusiasm for archaeological 'treasures', and especially the interest shown by Queen Caroline, the wife of Ferdinand I of Naples, was halted by political instability and popular uprisings in the city: ominous echoes of the French Revolution. After the flight of the Bourbons, the area remained under Napoleonic rule until 1815. The new French king of Naples, Joaquin Murat, supervised the excavations at Pompeii, but systematic work was only undertaken after the return of the Bourbons. The most exciting discoveries at that time were of houses associated with illustrious citizens.

Francois Gérard, *Portrait of Murat*, King of Naples. Spalletti Collection, Ravenna. Murat became king after the exile of the Bourbons and took an active interest in the excavations at Pompeii.

Egyptian obelisk in Piazza del Popolo, Rome, erected by Domenico Fontana in about 1593.

Domenico Fontana, Architect and Engineer

The first sporadic finds were unearthed in Pompeii at the end of the 16th century, following Domenico Fontana's development work in the Sarno valley. At that time there was no clear distinction between architects and engineers as their roles frequently overlapped. The few talented men engaged on developments inside and outside the cities were expected to make them more attractive as well as to devise practical solutions, such as roads, aqueducts and ports, in order to improve the lives of their inhabitants. Domenico Fontana, born in 1543 on Lake Lugano, was engaged initially on the grandiose building projects devised by Pope Sixtus V in Rome, and later on developments in the Kingdom of Naples. He was fully employed in Rome until the death of Sixtus V, in 1593: he planned the dramatic Via Sistina and devised the network of roads around Trajan's Column, Piazza del Popolo, and St John Lateran: he also erected obelisks in the last two sites. He worked in Naples from 1593 until his death in 1607. There too he built new roads, worked on the royal palace, and was engaged on aqueduct and canal developments outside the city. It was while engaged on a project in the Sarno valley that he was the first to discover the remains of Pompeii.

Statue of Hermes from the Villa of the Papyrus, or Pisoni, Herculaneum. National Archeological Museum, Naples.

THE DISCOVERY OF HERCULANEUM

Excavations under the Bourbon king Charles III were also undertaken in Herculaneum. In 1748 work was entrusted to the military engineer Joaquin de Alcubierre, described by the celebrated art historian Winckelmann as *'a man who knew as much about archaeology as the moon does about shrimps'*. Together with Karl Weber and the accomplished draughtsman, Francesco La Vega, Alcubierre used a pickaxe to dig out underground tunnels, known as the 'Bourbon warrens', solely designed to retrieve works of art. In 1750 the Villa of the Papyrus was discovered more than 20 metres underground. During these excavations of Herculaneum, lasting some ten years, magnificent statues in marble and bronze were discovered together with 2,000 fragments of half-carbonised papyrus.

14 POMPEII

View of the excavations with the modern city of Herculaneum in the background.

The king of Naples created the Portici Museum to house the statues, and founded the Herculaneum Academy. Strict restrictions were imposed on visits to the sites, even those by experts and scholars who had come from abroad to admire the buried city. Despite the success of the excavations they were temporarily interrupted after protests when contemporary houses collapsed as a result of the works.

Naples in the 18th Century

In the 18th century many eyes – and unfortunately a large number of hands – fixed on the treasures of Naples: Austrians, French, Spanish, and Republicans all fought to gain control over the lively, creative and cosmopolitan. During this period the porcelain museum of Capodimonte was founded together with the San Carlo opera house and the Accademia Ercolanense, housing all the major finds from the area surrounding Vesuvius. The king, although no connoisseur, understood that patronage was essential to the creation of a great city. During the reign of Ferdinand I (1751–1825), mostly through the intervention of his wife Marie Caroline of Austria, the arts were encouraged and collectors and intellectuals played a determining role in the cultural development of the city.

Frontispiece
of F. Mazois'
*The Ruins
of Pompeii.*

François Mazois

Scholars and enthusiasts, who
patiently drew and catalogued
the paintings, mosaics
and objects unearthed at
Herculaneum and Pompeii
(many of which were later
stolen by treasure seekers),
greatly increased awareness of
the marvels being discovered.

Many French visitors, for
the most part architects and
engravers, provided detailed
documentation of the sites.

Chief among these was
François Mazois (1783–1826),
who left some 450 fine
drawings of monuments
and buildings, detailed plans
of houses and intriguing
hypothetical reconstructions of
other structures and furniture.

The Italian painter Francesco
Morelli also worked on a
vast body of watercolours of
Pompeii in 1811.

Anton Raphael
Mengs, *Portrait
of Johann
Joachim
Winckelmann.*
Metropolitan
Museum of Art,
New York.

JOHANN JOACHIM WINCKELMANN

The German scholar
Winckelmann moved to
Rome after his conversion
to Catholicism to become
librarian and keeper of
antiquities to Cardinal Albani
in 1758. A self-taught expert
on archaeology, he travelled
to Herculaneum in 1762,
publishing his *Letter to Count
Brühl on the discoveries of
Herculaneum* in the same
year. In Naples he was given
permission to study the
collection of antique sculpture,
but he was denied access to
the excavations. Winckelmann
only succeeded in getting
into Herculaneum by bribing
the guards and was furious
that the discoveries were
kept so secret. In 1764 he
published a report accusing
the authorities of pilfering
and undertaking an arbitrary
programme of restoration.

Winckelmann, the author
of *The History of Ancient
Art* and of *Beauty and Art,* is
now considered the founder
of scientific archaeology,
even though he failed to
recognize a number of fakes.

Travellers and Artists

In the 18th and 19th centuries Herculaneum and Pompeii attracted artists and men of letters from all over Europe: scholars, collectors or the merely curious. In 1740 Horace Walpole strolled through Herculaeum in *'great wonder'*.

Later, in the first half of the 19th century, Stendhal visited the excavations at Pompeii some eleven times *'with extreme pleasure'*, and felt *'transported into antiquity'*.

Goethe and the painter Johann Heinrich Wilhelm Tischbein arrived in Naples in 1787 where they were denied permission to draw on the sites. Only after a prolonged wrangle were they allowed to record selected areas in the presence of a guard.

Despite this rather hostile reception, in his *Italian Journey* Goethe described his visit with a mixture of admiration, wonder and anguish for the *'mummified city'* Tischbein wrote in his memoirs of *'the most important revelations about painting'* experienced in Herculaeum and Pompeii.

Another German painter, Jakob-Philipp Hackert, court painter to Ferdinand I of Naples from 1786, was granted unrestricted access to the marvels of Pompeii and Herculaneum.

Bronze coin with a portrait of Goethe, from the British Museum, London. The German poet was one of the most celebrated visitors to Pompeii and Herculaneum in the 18th and 19th centuries.

Opposite: *Sacrifice of Iphigenia*, National Archaeological Museum, Naples. Wall paintings like this one inspired artists throughout the 18th and 19th centuries.

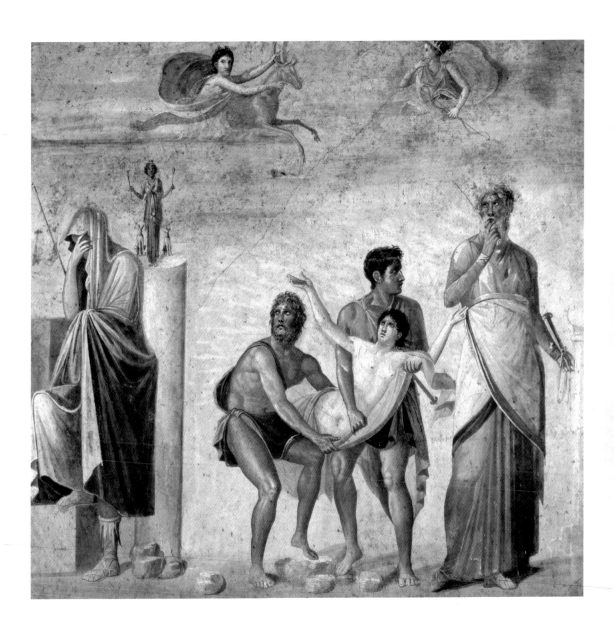

The Pompeian Style

In the mid-18th century the archaeologist and collector Conte de Caylus (1692–1765), having read the descriptions of the excavations by the Abbé Le Blanc, decided to publish his own book of 'discoveries' made up of highly imaginative drawings done 'from memory' as he had not been allowed to make notes or sketches. The *Antiquities of Herculaneum* included 700 paintings, 350 statues, 700 vases, 40 candelabras, 800 manuscripts and 600 assorted objects. It aroused enormous interest in France and was used as a manual by artists, goldsmiths, interior decorators and craftsmen who referred to it in their designs for furniture and furnishings.

Architecture and painting were not immediately influenced by the Pompeian style, although it later inspired the decoration of walls at Capodimonte and the pictures with putti by Vien and Canova. But even more than drawing inspiration from the Roman styles, artists were fascinated by recreating the scene of the eruption itself and the desperate flight of the inhabitants amid chaos and destruction. In 1834 the extremely popular *Last Days of Pompeii* by Bulwer-Lytton appeared. From the late 19th century, when America became gripped by news of the ancient cities, until quite recently, the Pompeian style in architecture was in vogue.

For example, the terraces, pool and sculptures of the Getty Museum in Malibu, completed in 1974, were modelled on the Villa of the Papyrus and, the 18th century drawings by Karl Weber.

Giovacchino Toma, *Fall of ash from Vesuvius.* Gallery of Modern Art, Florence. The eruption which buried Pompeii and Herculaneum was a constant source of fascination to artists.

The history of the excavations at Pompeii changed radically after the formation of the Kingdom of Italy. In 1860 Pompeii and Herculaneum were entrusted to the archaeologist and numismatist Giuseppe Fiorelli, who conducted operations according to rigid scientific principles. He divided the city of Pompeii into areas he called 'Islands' and 'Regions' (*Insulae* and *Regiones*) and assigned them numbers still in use today.

Fiorelli blocked the hasty dismantling of wall paintings and mosaics, and began restoration *in situ* creating a precise inventory of the whole site: plans were drawn up and paintings and objects copied. From 1860 systematic excavations began with new techniques which, although not as advanced as those adopted in the 20th century,

Wall painting of a *putto* on a chariot, about 60 AD, from the House of the Vettii, Pompeii. The systematic excavations begun by Fiorelli led to the discovery, study and restoration of many paintings and mosaics.

Cast of one
of the victims
of Vesuvius,
Pompeii.

The Plaster Casts:
an Invention of the
Archaeologist Fiorelli

Giuseppe Fiorelli had casts
made by pouring liquid plaster
into the cavities formed by
the carbonised bodies to
recreate not only the shapes
of Pompeii's inhabitants but
also everyday objects such
as doors, wooden staircases
and furniture. But the figures
are the most striking, caught
in their attempt to escape or
shelter from the falling rocks:
their poses are desperate as
they huddle, lie prone on the
ground, kneel or try to protect
their children. In the grounds
of one house later known as
the 'garden of the fleeing',
the remains of more than
ten victims were discovered,
probably asphyxiated by the
noxious gases. Some of these
19th century casts are on
display in the Antiquarium: at
first glance they appear to be
real bodies covered in grey
mud.

Giuseppe Fiorelli

Giuseppe Fiorelli, who was
Director of Works from
1860 to 1875, revolutionized
operations on the sites.
Pompeii became a vast
research laboratory where
new excavation and
restoration techniques were
put into practice. Fiorelli,
who was well aware of his
responsibilities, drew up the
first large plan of Pompeii,
had a model of the city made,
and collected some 1,200
documents relating to past
excavations.

were a great improvement
on earlier methods. In 1863
Giuseppe Fiorelli also became
director of what had become
the National Museum in
Naples, and devoted his time
to compiling monumental
volumes on Pompeii, including
*A Report on the excavations
at Pompeii from 1861 to 1872*,
published in 1873, and the
Description of Pompeii, in
1875. During his directorship
imprints of human and animal
bodies were discovered at
Pompeii recording the position
of the victims when disaster
struck in 79 AD. Their shapes
were left imbedded in the
hot ash, which had hardened
around the bodies. The
problem was: how to preserve
these vital records? Fiorelli
decided to have casts made
and therefore gave form to
these people and animals who
had perished centuries before
in their desperate attempt
to escape the eruption.

Opposite: Casts
of figures from
Pompeii caught
in the moment
of death at
the time of

the eruption
of Vesuvius in
79 AD. Pompeii.
Fiorelli was the
first to discover
the imprints

made by the
bodies and have
plaster casts
made.

Excavations in
Pompeii in
about 1870.

Discoveries in the 20th Century

Fiorelli's work was continued by his colleagues Michele Ruggiero and Giulio de Petra, who succeeded in stabilizing most of the buildings. In the period between 1906 and 1910 some splendid houses were unearthed, the House of the Vettii among them. Techniques continually improved from the early 20th century, making it possible to excavate whole buildings intact, including the ceilings. This was rare in the history of archaeology, as normally sites are mapped out on the basis of foundations or low surviving walls with very few high structures. Until 1923 Vittorio Spinazzola worked on the old city centre and the shops in Pompeii. From the following year until the 1960s the archaeologist Amedeo Maiuri sought to establish stricter controls for the protection and conservation of the whole area. Work was

Via delle tombe, or the 'road of the tombs', seen from Porta Nocera. This area was excavated in the second half of the 20th century under Amedeo Maiuri.

The provisions market (*macellum*) in the forum, Pompeii. Many of the buildings in this area suffered during the 1980 earthquake.

The Earthquake

In 1980, after some 66 hectares of Pompeii, or two thirds of the whole site had been brought to light, a violent earthquake struck. It destabilized walls and columns and damaged 600 houses. Three years later the French national scientific research institute C.N.R.S. published an assessment of the damage and proposed a programme of restoration.

Generous financial aid was forthcoming and a special commission 'Pompeii Project' was set up: unfortunately the funds allotted by the EU were blocked for 'administrative' reasons. Individual monuments such as the city baths and *Insulae* received attention, but much more was needed. Cracks, collapses and scaffolding bear witness to the continual difficulties facing the city. Recently several areas have been restored: in 2004 the wall paintings in the shops on Via dell'Abbondanza were conserved and the buildings on the Lupanare were strengthened.

Amedeo Maiuri

Amedeo Maiuri (1886-1963) carried out extensive work in the field, determined as he was not only to bring the monuments of old Pompeii to light but also to reveal the complex city structure both within and outside the eight gates of the city walls. He published innumerable scholarly texts, guides and catalogues.

But the uncontrolled growth of modern Pompeii infringed increasingly on the excavations and he was forced to retreat inside the original perimeter.

interrupted during World War II when the site was partially damaged by bombs.

Excavations were resumed after the war: in 1951 the city walls and the necropolis in via Nocera were discovered.

Other finds outside the city walls created a more complete picture of the original urban complex. North of Pompeii, at Boscoreale, two villas were found, first unearthed between 1897 and 1900 and later fully excavated. Today little remains of them apart from a large number of household objects, including some vases and pieces in silver now in the Louvre and a number of paintings dispersed throughout the world's museums: in Naples, the Metropolitan in New York, in Brussels, Paris and Amsterdam. In 1964 work began on the richly decorated villa of Poppea at Oplontis, now Torre Annunziata.

Silver beaker
with skeletons,
now at the
Louvre,
Paris. This
and similarly
splendid objects
were found at
Boscoreale, a
site unearthed
at the beginning
of the 20th
century to the
north
of Pompeii.

View of the *triclinium* *from the* Villa of Poppea Oplontis. The excavation of this villa, discovered in 1964, gave new insight into the villas surrounding Pompeii.

THE MYSTERIES OF POMPEII: DIONYSIAN RITUAL IN THE VILLA OF THE MYSTERIES

Wall paintings of about 50 AD from the Villa of the Mysteries, Pompeii, howing mysterious rituals.

Among the many houses brought to light by Maiuri, the beautiful Villa of the Mysteries *(Villa dei Misteri)* has remained a source of wonder and debate on account of the

magnificent but mysterious wall paintings in the *triclinium*. The Villa is to the west of the old city outside the walls. It is a complex structure, originating in the early years of the 2nd century BC, which was enlarged and rebuilt several times. Although originally a private house, in the 1st century AD it was transformed into a flourishing farm with equipment for making wine and oil. The area for wine production is particularly well preserved with vats for

Wall painting showing purification rites, from the Villa of the Mysteries. Some female figures prepare a bath in the presence of a satyr.

pressing the grapes and a large container for the must. But the paintings remain the most remarkable feature of the villa. The *triclinium* houses the most celebrated cycle in the city with large figures shown against a background of 'Pompeian' red: they appear to be undergoing some sort of initiation rite, but interpretation is difficult.

On the left wall, a group with a young boy reading in the presence of two matrons is shown with a second group made up exclusively of women who are preparing a bath. There follows a satyr leaning on a pilaster, a group of lovers in a rustic setting and a female figure fleeing in fright. On the next wall, after a group with Silenus and satyrs showing a mask, Dionysus and Ariadne appear with the unveiling of a phallus by semi-naked girls in the presence of a winged creature. On the last wall, a frightened girl seeks comfort in the lap of a matron, with a *toilette* scene in the presence of Eros

Wall painting of Silenus, satyrs, Dionysus and Ariadne, from the Villa of the Mysteries. The presence of Dionysus adds weight to the theory that the scenes refer to a mysterious cult.

40 POMPEII

and a bejewelled matron.

The ritual and sacred mood in these paintings is palpable and the figures are made more striking depicted against the red ground. The most widely accepted interpretation is that the scenes represent Dionysian initiation rites, widely diffused in the Roman world and opposed by the official religion: they were deemed subversive and bent on overthrowing public order. Every scene represents a different aspect of the cult: the first would be the receipt of the letter and the preparation of the ritual bath, followed by the revelation of the mask and the phallus (symbol of the regenerative powers of nature), then the winged demon and the kneeling woman, to be interpreted as flagellation scenes. Everything takes place in the presence of deities such as Pan and Silenus, accompanied by satyrs and dancing maidens. Another

interpretation suggests that the paintings are copies of a Hellenistic wedding cycle: the Roman copyist has simplified and corrupted the original version. The bride prepares her *toilette* with the help of her mother, followed by the preparation of the ritual bath and the reading of the wedding contract in the presence of the divinities Dionysus and Ariadne. There are others who read the paintings as Dionysian satire: the scene with the letter would allude to the childhood of the god, the figure carrying a tray and the three women seated around the table are seen as personifications of the seasons; the young woman weeping in the lap of a matron refers to Semele giving birth to Dionysus.

In this interpretation the unveiled phallus becomes a threat to Nemesis (the winged demon), who was sent by Hera, offended at the birth of Dionysus by her rival Semele.

Wall painting showing the unveiling of a phallic symbol and a winged demon from the Villa of the Mysteries. The unveiling of a phallus was a crucial part of ritual orgies.

Wall painting
from the Villa of
the Mysteries
showing a bride
at her toilette.

Wall painting from the Villa of the Mysteries showing female figures and dancing maenads, 50 AD. The two figures of the left, linked by the winged demon depicted on the nearby wall, would appear to hint at a scene of ritual flagellation.

THE REMAINS OF A CIVILIZATION
POMPEII: DAILY LIFE

Mosaic of a gladiator, from the *palaestra* in Pompeii. National Archaeological Museum, Naples.

The dramatic way Pompeii was destroyed, a fate shared by the other cities below Vesuvius, has allowed us not only to 'uncover' and observe everyday details of life within the city, but also to construct a more complete picture of Roman civilization as a whole. We can see the temples where the Roman deities were worshipped, and the once-bustling streets lined with shops where ancient trades and crafts, in some cases almost unchanged today, were practised. We can revisit the public places, the arenas for political activity and for games; the baths and public exercise grounds *(palaestrae)* where hours were devoted to the care and relaxation of the body. Roman life is revealed to us in all its rich variety as it was at the very moment it was stilled in Pompeii in the August of 79 AD.

The Origins of Pompeii

View of
Vesuvius from
Mt. Faito.
The settlement
of Pompeii
was built
on a plateau
near
the volcano.

The history of Pompeii began many years before the birth of Christ when a plateau, only 30 metres above sea-level and crossed by the river Sarno, was first inhabited at the end of the 7th century BC. This early settlement was built on the solidified lava flow of a previous eruption of Vesuvius in a position of strategic importance. From their privileged position the first settlers were able to exploit

the natural resources of the area, control the major routes of communication, and have access to the sea. The fertile plain favoured agricultural production while the Sarno river provided fresh water.

The first inhabitants were of Oscan origin and language: the *Opici* or *Osci*, as they are described in the early sources, natives of the Campania region and the first people to leave significant archaeological traces in the area. Tombs provide the earliest signs of their existence from the 9th century BC.

Archaeological investigation has only recently begun to shed light on the earliest history of Pompeii. Before this little was known and much was conjecture, but now the first city walls have been unearthed together with the foundations of houses built in the 6th century BC.

At this stage there was at least one wall surrounding the city, roughly coinciding with the extent of the earlier

View of the ruins of Pompeii with a backdrop of Vesuvius. The volcano overshadowed daily life in the city before causing its destruction.

Part of the walls surrounding Pompeii, with a watch tower in the background. The first circle of the city walls was recently discovered.

lava flow. The fortifications were important as they suggest not only the need to defend the city from external danger but an advanced

political development within the settlement: to build a wall around a city requires a degree of social organization.

The Porta of Nola led out of Pompeii towards the Etruscan city of Nola.

The Expansion of the Etruscans into Campania

From the beginning of the first millennium BC, when the first urban settlements appeared in Etruria, the Etruscans also started to move northwards towards the Padana plains and south towards Campania. Here they established settlements at Capua and Pontecagnano, to the north of Naples. Objects from distant lands found in tombs in these places from the mid-9th century BC bear witness to long-established trading contacts with people beyond the sea.

The Etruscans wasted no time in making contact with the Greeks, especially with the *Euboici*, who shortly afterwards in the 8th century BC founded Pithekoussai (Ischia), the first Italian colony. In the 7th century BC Etruscan rule extended over Campania: we can trace the extent of their power in the use of the Etruscan language on surviving inscriptions. These were found in Etruscan centres such as Pontecagnano and Capua, as well as in settlements founded by native people like those at Pompeii and Stabia.

In Campania, the different cultures (indigenous, Etruscan, Greek) lived side by side and were culturally integrated, despite the frequent strain on diplomatic ties. Etruscan expansion was not of the colonial kind: it focused rather on creating close cultural and commercial links between Campania and Etruria.

The Etruscans at Pompeii

The cultural panorama of the Pompeii region in the 6th century BC is made more complex by the presence of the Etruscans.

Their expansion from present-day Tuscany to the north and south extended into Campania, the region around Pompeii. There they met local Italian colonies but also the Greeks who inhabited Ischia and Cuma.

As a result of their encounter with the Greeks, from the 8th century BC the Etruscans adopted major technical and cultural innovations such as writing, as well as Greek manners and customs including the drinking of wine during banquets, when vessels in the Greek style or even of Greek manufacture were used. Despite the Etruscans' adoption of many Greek customs, the two became political rivals.

The Greeks challenged the Etruscans' control over the coastal region in order to gain power over the local people.

Pompeii, then controlled by the Etruscans, lay between the Etruscan city of Nola and the coast dominated by the Greeks.

The ancient walls of the city were violently destroyed, perhaps in a military campaign by the Cumaen Greeks to counter Etruscan attempts to exploit the strategic importance of Pompeii against them.

Relations further degenerated in the second half of the 6th century BC when the Etruscans fought alongside the Carthaginians against the Greeks in the naval battle of Alalia (540 BC) in their struggle to gain control of the trade routes in the western Mediterranean.

In 524 BC the Etruscans attacked Cuma, in Campania, but failed to take the city, although their hold on Pompeii remained secure: numerous

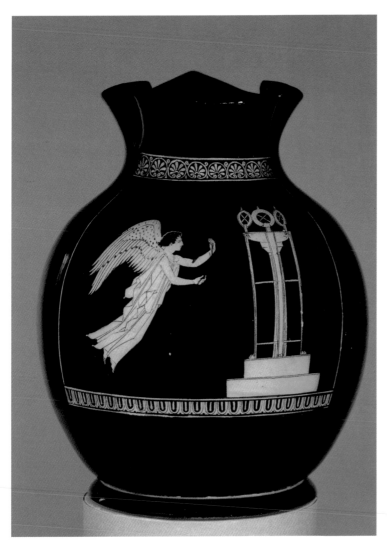

inscriptions in Etruscan bear witness to their occupation.

The Etruscan presence in Pompeii and neighbouring cities enlarged the community's cultural and commercial contacts.

Red-figure Attic *Oinochoe* discovered at Nola, 5 BC. Ashmolean Museum, Oxford. The Etruscan cities in the Campania came under Greek influence, apparent in the numerous Hellenic objects unearthed in the area.

Vase from Eubea, 8th century BC. Archaeological Museum, Athens. The inhabitants of Eubea were the founders of the Greek colonies at Cuma and Pithekoussai.

Greek Colonization in Campania

The process of 'colonization', embarked on by the Greeks from the 8th century BC in southern Italy and Sicily, would appear to have been motivated by the search for more fertile land. But although this was clearly a bonus enjoyed by the settlers, archaeological evidence indicates that commercial interests were the motivational force driving colonization.

The Greeks established their first colonies not in prime agricultural areas but in those closest to the Etruscans who were the most dynamic people in southern Italy at that time. In the 8th century BC they therefore established colonies at Pithekoussai (Ischia) and at Cuma in Campania.

These colonists came from Eubea, and were already well known as traders along the Italian coast especially on the shores of the Tyrrhenian. Cuma in turn established a further settlement in Naples–*nea-polis* in Greek means new city.

Close ties between the Greeks and Etruscans, led to the Etruscan adoption of the Greek Euboen alphabet, then handed down to the Latin people. Cultural exchanges and a certain reciprocal understanding resulted from these commercial relations, the main source of wealth in the Mediterranean at the time.

The Greek Influence

After the foundation of the first Greek colonies in Campania in the 8th century BC Greek influence in the region increased enormously, including the spread of Greek cults and religious beliefs.

Temples were built to Greek gods even outside centres controlled by the Greeks. At Pompeii for example the cult of Apollo was introduced.

He was the god of poetry and music but was also a shepherd and warrior, the inspiration of philosophical thought and provider of moral and legal guidance. The temple dedicated to Apollo is still visible at the entrance to the Civic Forum, coming from the Porta Marina. The statue of the god found in fragments in the west of the city probably came from this temple.

From the 6th century BC various sanctuaries were dedicated to Apollo in other Etruscan cities in Campania and also in Pyrgi, and in Etruria itself. Small communities of

Greek merchants, resident in Etruscan cities, probably sought protection from Apollo as they were in the minority. The buildings certainly bear witness to the cultural exchange and degree of religious toleration between the two peoples, who both sought to maintain commercial interests in the Mediterranean, especially in the Tyrrhenian Sea.

The temple of Apollo, 2nd century BC, Pompeii. The cult of Apollo was introduced to the Campania region when the earliest Greek colonies were founded.

From Samnite to
Roman Domination

Detail of the *impluvium* from the mid-1st century BC, Samnite House, Pompeii. The building is named after the Samnites who settled in Pompeii in the 4th century BC.

At the end of the 5th century BC the Samnites, powerful warriors from the mountainous hinterland of Campania, Molise and the Abruzzi, left their strongholds and moved towards the coast in search of more fertile land. Their arrival, which probably coincided with local insurrections, signalled the end of Etruscan power in Campania. The Samnites also took control of Pompeii, attracted by its favourable coastal position on a fertile plain near the

mouth of the Sarno river.

During the 4th century BC the city, with a mixed Samnite and local population, saw a remarkable growth. Important public buildings were erected in the historic centre and the number of private houses greatly increased: the Forum was built and remained little changed under the Romans.

The Samnites too became engaged in the commerce already practised by the Carthaginians and Romans: trading centres all along the Mediterranean coast increased and thrived.

Rome made a series of trade agreements with the Carthaginians, to divide the spoils of the Mediterranean

trade while at the same time hoping to maintain good relations with the Samnite confederation: by the 4th century BC the Samnites had expanded from coast to coast across the Apennines.

In 354 BC a treaty was signed between the Romans and the Samnites aimed at defining their spheres of influence, followed in 348 BC by the renewal of the previous agreement between Rome and Carthage.

A few years later, however, the Roman senate decided to intervene on the part of the other Italic people in Campania against the Samnites: the first Samnite war fought between 343 and 341 BC was something of a stalemate.

The Romans were forced to return to Lazio to put down an uprising closer to home and had to abandon their military ambitions in Campania.

Road leading into the Forum at Pompeii, about 120 BC. The Forum was first laid out under the Samnites.

Wall painting
from a tomb on
the Esquiline
Hill in Rome,
showing
episodes from
the second
Samnite
war, end 4th
century BC.
Capitoline
Museum, Rome.

Having re-established hold over the cities of Lazio, Rome turned south again, attacked Naples and fought the second Samnite war from 326 to 304 BC. They extended the conflict into Puglia where they gained allies in the cities of Lucera and Canosa but in 321 BC were forced into the humiliating surrender of the Forche Caudine. In 305 BC the Romans once again advanced on Puglia and the Samnite territories with the aim of

taking their most important city of Boiano. Forced to make peace, the Samnites maintained their independence but were no longer the supreme power in Campania, the Abruzzi and Puglia.

The third Samnite war was fought between 298 and 290 BC by a coalition of the Samnite and other people, including the Etruscans, Gauls, Sabines, Lucans, Umbrians and Picenes. In 295 BC at Sentino in Umbria the Romans at last gained a decisive but bloody victory, although peace was not finally made with the determined Samnites until 290 BC. At this point southern Italy came firmly under Roman control.

From the end of the 5th to the beginning of the 3rd century BC the Samnites and other Italic peoples, having overthrown Etruscan supremacy, maintained their hold over a large part of Campania, with Pompeii as a strategic point. It was only the persistent efforts of the Roman army which finally crushed Samnite power in the area.

Associates and Citizens: Rights and Duties of the Subject People

In Roman political organization, during the period of the Republic, those designated as citizens, (even if they were not from Rome) were granted all the rights guaranteed by the laws of Rome. The citizen, the *civis*, was protected by the law, while having certain duties with regard to the state including the payment of taxes and military service.

The Republic incorporated numerous defeated and subject cities: these often became *municipi*.

The *municipia optimo iure* (municipalities with suffrage) enjoyed full Roman citizenship; the *municipia sine suffragio* (without suffrage) had civic rights but not political ones. Allies and associates were those peoples and communities allied to Rome by a treaty, either by their own volition or following a military defeat.

The treaties between Rome and her associates varied: some offered almost equal rights and obligations to both parties (*foedera aequa* = equal agreements); others, especially when imposed after military defeat, were much more advantageous to the Romans (*foedera iniqua* = unequal agreements).

All the associates maintained administrative independence together with a local magistrature. Although internal politics remained independent these communities were obliged to support Rome's policy of aggrandizement by supplying soldiers to the army.

The Stabian Baths, Pompeii, built under the Samnites.

The Via di Stabia,
constructed under
the Samnites.
Pompeii.

Pompeii ended up under
Roman dominion, becoming
an 'associate', which allowed
the city a relative degree
of local autonomy, before
becoming in the 1st century
BC a *municipium*, whose
inhabitants enjoyed the same
rights as Roman citizens.

The Birth of the Roman Colony

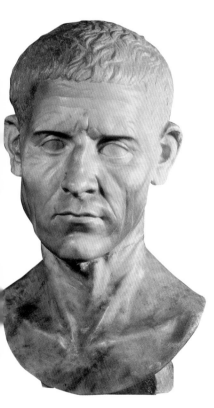

Supposed portrait of Sulla from the middle of the 1st century BC. Archaeological Museum, Venice. Sulla crushed the rebellion of Pompeii.

Between the end of the 2nd and beginning of the 1st century BC the Roman associates and the Italic cities became increasingly unhappy with the economic and social conditions their position imposed. More importantly the strain of military service to Rome and her allies was becoming intolerable. The associates began agitating for better treatment and claimed the same rights as Roman citizens. These guaranteed a number of advantages and privileges denied to mere allies. In 95 BC a revolt in the Piceno and the Samnite lands extended rapidly through southern Italy and into Cisalpine Gaul and Etruria: it was known as the Social War as it was begun by the *soci* (or allies) against Rome.

This war was hardly ever fought on open ground, but was made up of a series of sporadic attacks on terrain chosen to put the Romans at a disadvantage. In 89 BC resistance was still maintained in Sannio, Nola, Lucania and in Bruzio. In Campania few cities remained loyal to Rome after nearly all the major cities rebelled. In the same year the port of Stabia, of great strategic importance to the rebels, was razed to the ground by Lucius Cornelius Sulla, the great Roman general and statesman. He then advanced on Pompeii: in 89 BC the city was besieged and brought back under the aegis of Rome. The defeated inhabitants fled to Nola where the city denied them exile: the rebels were then slaughtered by the Roman army.

Pompeii was spared and turned into a Roman colony. In 80 BC it was named *Colonia Cornelia Veneria Pompeiianorum*, in homage

to Sulla (Cornelio) and Venus, the patron goddess of the city. Land was confiscated and granted to veterans who had fought with Sulla.

Families and political groups who had given Sulla their support gained control of key posts in the city while the previous officials were turned out in disgrace. Despite these dramatic changes the city continued to prosper and expanded still further.

Statue of Venus, patron goddess of the Roman colony in Pompeii, now kept in the Antiquarium there.

The Beginning
of the Imperial Age

The amphitheatre at Pompeii, about 70 BC. This and other typically Roman public buildings were constructed after the foundation of the Roman colony.

In the urban development of Pompeii there was considerable continuity with the pre-colonial period.

After the constitution of the *Colonia Cornelia* the new buildings included the amphitheatre on the eastern extremity of the city and the new baths in the Forum.

These developments were in harmony with previous buildings, as public entertainment and thermal centres were extremely important throughout the

Augustus of Prima Porta, 8 BC. Vatican Palace, Rome. The reign of Augustus put an end to long years of war and ushered in a period of great splendour.

cities in Campania.

Other changes seemed more associated with the Roman way of life, such as the importance of the cult of Venus: a sanctuary was built in the colony dedicated to her.

The beginning of the Empire witnessed a whole spate of public building. New road networks, drains, and acqueducts appeared all over Campania.

After the battle of Azio (31 BC) and the victory of Augustus, who became emperor in 27 BC a period of almost perpetual warfare was brought to an end.

There then followed years of increasing prosperity with lavish expenditure on public works, not only in Rome. Under the Augustan reforms Campania was incorporated into Lazio to become a single region, the *Regio I*: roadways improved dramatically.

An aqueduct was brought to Pompeii so that the inhabitants no longer had to rely on cisterns and wells to store rain or extract

Paved road with pavements for pedestrians in Pompeii. Extensive road building was carried out under Augustus.

Opposite: Garden with a nympheum and a canal, Pompeii. Under Augustus water was brought to the city by an aqueduct.

water from superficial springs. The aqueduct, built on Augustus's orders, stretched for hundreds of kilometres across Campania.

With the arrival of water

fountains, nympheums and public laundries appeared in the city and villas and private homes were clearly improved by the abundant supply.

A Violent Earthquake

Painting showing the riot of 59 AD in the amphitheatre at Pompeii. National Archaeological Museum,

Painting showing the riot of 59 AD in the amphitheatre at Pompeii. National Archaeological Museum, Naples. This disturbance in 59 AD resulted in the Pompeians killing supporters from Nuceria.

The inhabitants of Pompeii enjoyed the good life. Ugly incidents such as the riot in the ampitheatre between the fans of Pompeii and Nuceria in 59 AD, when the visiting supporters were massacred, were rare. The impact made by the event is recorded in a wall-painting in a house in Pompeii. As a result of the riot Nero ordered the closure of the amphitheatre for the next ten years. After only three the city was hit by a catastrophic earthquake which destroyed many of the public buildings there and in the surrounding cities. A laborious reconstruction was begun, but the extent of the damage forced many of the inhabitants to seek refuge in villas in the nearby countryside. The scale of the operation and quite possibly corruption hampered progress so that after 15 years some buildings were not yet complete: these included the buildings around the Forum and the temple of Jupiter.

The Emperor Titus:
a Troubled Reign

Seventeen years after the disastrous earthquake, while the city was still undergoing reconstruction, the dramatic and quite unexpected eruption of Vesuvius brought life in the city to an end. Many of the city's inhabitants were buried under metres of ash and stone while those who managed to escape lost all their worldly goods.

In the year when Pompeii was lost the Emperor Titus, the son of Vespasian, also came to the throne. The new emperor had a reputation for cruelty: during his father's

reign he had violently put down the revolt in Judea and destroyed the temple in Jerusalem in August 70 AD.

The eruption of Vesuvius in 79 AD was not a good omen. Nevertheless Titus proved to be a wise ruler, both moderate and enlightened, although his reign only lasted two years. Following the destruction of Pompeii there was also a fire in Rome which brought widespread damage to the city. On his death in 81 AD Titus was mourned by the people of Rome.

Statue of Titus in a toga, about 80 AD. Vatican Palace, Rome. Titus came to the throne in the same year as Pompeii and Herculaneum were destroyed.

The City Buried
by Vesuvius

On 24 August, 79 AD, a dense cloud of smoke gave warning of the impending disaster. This was shortly followed by a shower of rocks and stones from the volcano with fires being sparked off in the plain below. Ash then piled up on the roads and houses, already destabilized by the previous earthquake.

There was a strong smell of sulphur everywhere. Many who managed to escape the initial damage of the eruption and the falling rocks were asphyxiated by the thick smoke and fumes. Pliny the

Karl Pawlowitsch Brjullow, *The last day of Pompeii*. Detail. Russian State Museum, St Petersburg.

The Account of Pliny the Younger

A vivid account was left by Pliny the Younger (61–112 AD), who was only 17 at the time: *'Ash was already falling on the boats, which became hotter and thicker the closer one came towards land; pumice and rocks of fire were also falling from the sky. From many points flames and the light of fires were visible, made more dramatic by the darkness of the night. The sea appeared to be drawn in on itself as though repelled by an earthquake. From over part of the earth moved a frightening black cloud lit by occasional flashes of fire, spread in long streaks of flame, like lightning, but much more terrifying. You could hear the screams of women, the cries of children and men shouting [...] there were those for fear of death who called out its name. Many raised their arms to the gods, many cried out that the gods were dead, that eternal night had come, the last night of the world [...]. At last the eruption ceased leaving nothing but smoke and cloud. Daybreak came at last and the sun also shone, but it was pale like in an eclipse. And to our untrained eyes everything appeared changed, and covered in ash like a veil of snow.'*

Cast of one of the victims of Vesuvius in 79 AD. Pompeii.

Younger, nephew of the great naturalist and writer Pliny the Elder, admiral of the fleet at Misenum, provided an eye-witness account of the disaster. He described the terror of the inhabitants, their cries and desperation, the darkness, and the continual fall of ash burying the whole city.

Urban Development

The preservation of Pompeii following the eruption of Vesuvius allows us to study in extraordinary detail the structure of a Roman city. Even though Pompeii was of minor importance compared to the metropolis of Rome, it shared many of its characteristics. In Pompeii the local aristocracy, which was made up of wealthy landowners and rich merchants, lived in grand houses, often built on an enormous scale and sometimes set in panoramic positions on terraced ground.

These homes included reception rooms, loggias and large halls leading into gardens. Many houses also had shops facing the street, for the most part rented out or else run by slaves, where produce from the estate was sold. Craftsmen, small tradesmen and freemen lived in smaller houses: these had a gallery surrounding the rooms on the first floor. The careful distribution of space within these homes is indicative of the high cost of land suitable for building on.

The urban development of the city became much more complex during the Samnite period when the Civic Forum was built. At this time a large number of public buildings were completed and private houses, especially more luxurious ones, grew up rapidly. The city wall with gates was finished: later alterations to this wall did not alter the basic arrangement of the streets in the centre.

Splendid new buildings were constructed under the Romans, who also restored the earlier ones. During the Imperial age, and notably under the Julian-Claudian dynasty, Pompeii became particularly magnificent.

Among the other buildings dating from this period are the large public exercise grounds (*palaestrae*) and the temple of Fortuna Augusta.

After the earthquake in 62 AD the reconstruction of public and private buildings began, but progress was very slow especially with regard to the public ones. Many were still unfinished when the eruption of 79 AD put an end to any further hope of recovery.

View of the Forum, the centre of public life in the city, constructed in about 120 BC.

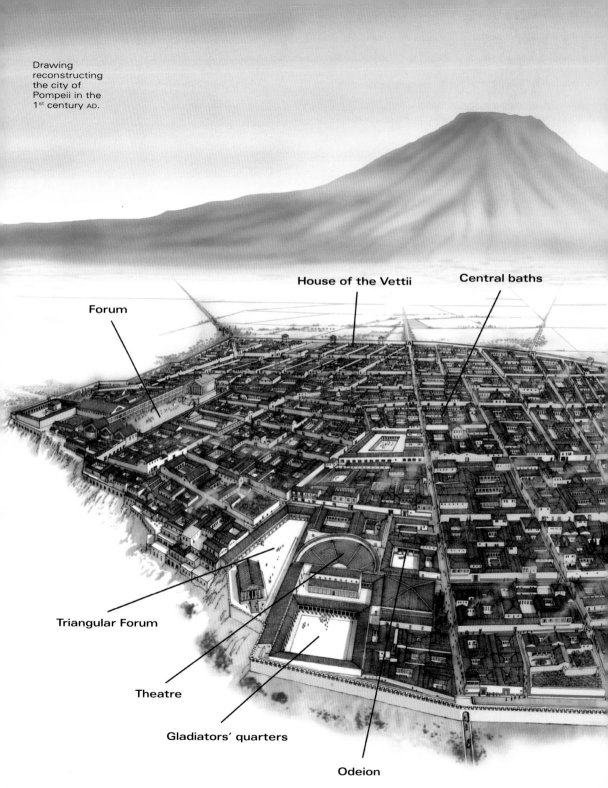

Drawing
reconstructing
the city of
Pompeii in the
1ˢᵗ century AD.

Forum

House of the Vettii

Central baths

Triangular Forum

Theatre

Gladiators' quarters

Odeion

Amphitheatre

Large Palestra

Private Houses:
Spatial Arrangement

Atrium of the House of Menander, dating from about 35 BC, in Pompeii. At the centre is the *impluvium* where rain water was gathered; smaller rooms open on both sides.

The layout of the private houses in Pompeii reflected the social standing of the inhabitants. Houses between the fourth and third centuries BC followed a clearly recognizable 'Italic' model, with rooms arranged around the atrium or hall. In the 2nd century BC the houses were enlarged with additions echoing the Greek style. The houses of the very poor were divided into tiny compartments and often served as workshops too, opening directly onto the street.

Internal space in the larger houses was arranged around the vestibule or entrance, linking the internal and external areas of the home. The vestibule led into the atrium, a hall and reception area built on a square plan with columns. It was covered by a roof which allowed sunlight and rainwater to enter. At the

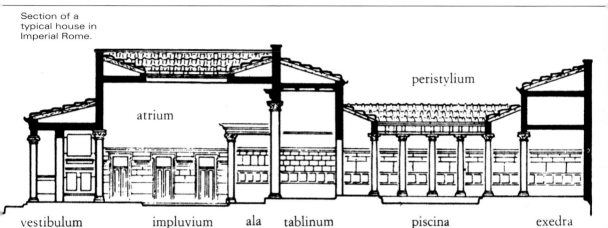

Section of a typical house in Imperial Rome.

peristylium

atrium

vestibulum   impluvium   ala   tablinum   piscina   exedra

centre was the *impluvium*, a rectangular basin for storing the rainwater from the gutters, which also replenished the house cistern. Off the atrium there was generally a room to house the household shrine (*lararium*), housing the gods who watched over the family.

The *tablinum* was for everday living and was often decorated with particular care. Sleep and rest was reserved for the *cubiculum* a dark and narrow space just off the atrium.

The *triclinium* was a dining area so named after the three couches arranged around a table for the comfort of the diners.

After came the serving rooms including the kitchen, larders, storerooms and baths. The peristyle was a colonnaded courtyard, an Hellenic import, around which the main rooms were arranged. Plants in the garden were laid out in a geometrical plan with a pool or pergola in the centre.

Sometimes a more elaborate shaded area was constructed in the garden to house the *triclinium* for banquets.

Cubiculum in the Villa of the Mysteries, about 50 BC. The bedroom (*cubiculum*) was usually close to the entrance of the house.

Large Public Buildings

The route from the Porta Marina to the Forum in Pompeii leads past a number of the most important public buildings. The basilica appears to date from the 2nd century BC and on its south-west corner opens onto the forum. Divided into three areas by rows of columns, it is a rectangular building and one of the most significant in the city, as it acted as the tribunal or law courts.

The Forum complex also included four temples, the provisions market (*macellum)* and the cloth traders hall (Eumachia building). This was dedicated as the inscription relates by the priestess Eumachia to the 'Concordia Augusta,' the peace conferred by Augustus. First built in the Samnite period, it was reconstructed under the Julian-Claudian dynasty when the tufo pavement was replaced by one in travertine marble. The temple of Apollo, begun in the 2nd century BC, stands on the south-west side of the Forum. It is fairly well conserved and it is possible to visit the *cella* – the inner precinct – which is raised on a platform with Corinthian columns at the front. The temple of Jupiter stands on the north side, opposite the *macellum*, with a high platform and double stairway and a cella divided into three by double rows of columns.

The temple, dedicated to the 'Capitoline trinity', (the 'official' Roman gods – Jupiter, Juno and Minerva), still shows sign of the damage suffered during the first earthquake in 62 AD, as by 79 AD restoration was not yet completed.

View of the Basilica, 2th century BC. Pompei.

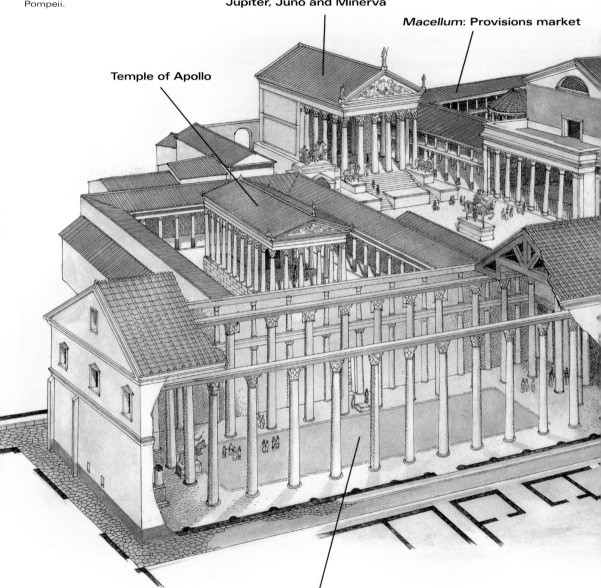

Reconstruction drawing showing the Forum in Pompeii.

Temple of the Capitoline Trinity:
Jupiter, Juno and Minerva

Macellum: Provisions market

Temple of Apollo

Basilica

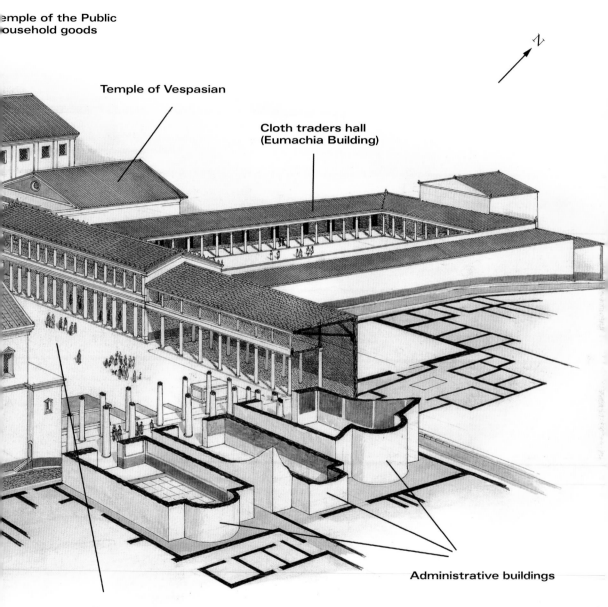

emple of the Public
ousehold goods

Temple of Vespasian

Cloth traders hall
(Eumachia Building)

Administrative buildings

Forum

Entertainment: the Amphiteatre and the Theatre

The amphiteatre in Pompeii was built by the Samnites in about 80 BC: it enclosed an immense arena where combat took place between gladiators and wild animals.

There were no rooms beneath the arena but traces survive of rooms designed above the *velarium*: an enormous canopy installed after the earthquake and used to shield the public from the rays of the sun or rain. There

View of the Pompeii amphitheatre, constructed in about 80 BC.

Wall painting showing a theatre, from Herculaneum. National Archaeological Museum, Naples. This wall painting gives a very clear idea of the original appearance and decoration of a Roman theatre.

Detail from a wall painting in Herculaneum, showing a theatrical mask. National Archaeological Museum, Naples.

Theatrical Performances

Satire (*satura*) is probably the oldest theatrical genre and it covered a vast array of subject matter. In about 300 BC the *atellana*, or Atellan Farce, was introduced to Rome, an improvised farce originally from Atella, in Campania.

The plot centres on intrigues, misunderstandings and accidents: the players wear masks. Livius Andronicus is supposed to have introduced Greek tragedy and comedy to Rome in the middle of the 3rd century BC. From the 1st century BC two new genres gained great popularity: mime and pantomime, the first usually comic and often ribald, the other tragic and frequently based on myth.

In these performances there were never more than three or four actors, always wearing the same mask: these made them easily identifiable to the public as the old man (*senex)*, the prostitute *(meretrice)*, the soldier (*miles*) and the servant (*servus*).

While in Rome the theatre was always recognised as an imported tradition, in Campania it was very much part of local culture, derived both from the Italic people and the Greeks. This explains the large number of theatres in the cities of the area.

is evidence of the restoration carried out after the 62 AD earthquake. A wall painting (now in the Naples Museum) showing the massacre of the supporters from Nuceria in the amphiteatre in 59 AD gives a very good idea of the original appearance of the space, with its high external walls built on a series of arches with two flights of steps leading to the upper level. In the south of the city, near the triangular Forum, are the Large Theatre with the nearby covered theatre or Odeon (*Odeum*). The remains of the Large Theatre, in the Greek style and probably dating to the 2nd century BC, suggest that it could have held as many as 5,000 spectators.

Now all that survives are the lower steps, reserved for the decurions, and part of the middle area, originally built on twenty rows, while there were four rows in the upper level. The stage was raised about a metre above the level of the orchestra and was reached by a flight of steps. A *quadriporticus* or loggia, hidden by a facade in imitation of a rich *palazzo*, was where the spectators withdrew during the interval.

The small odeon (housing about a thousand spectators), not far from the Large Theatre, was where concerts, performances, poetry and mime were held. The odeon is distinctive for its permanent roof cover, an unsupported span of some 20 metres.

Mosaic showing a tragic and a comic mask, 2nd century AD. Rome, Capitoline Museums. These two masks refer to the theatre.

Mosaic showing actors rehearsing a performance. National Archaeological Museum, Naples. Masks are also in evidence in this scene.

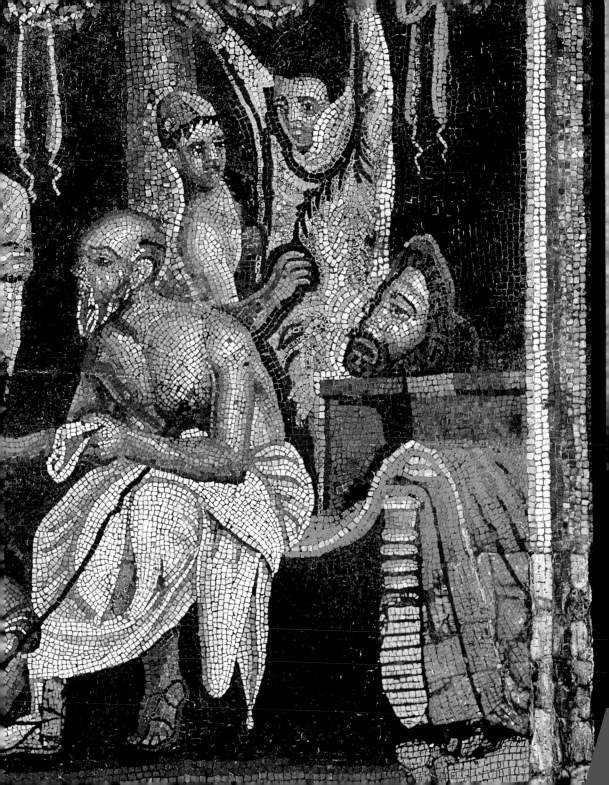

The Baths

There were as many as three public baths in Pompeii, open to both men and women.

They bear witness to the popularity of these centres throughout the whole Roman period. Visitors, having paid an entrance fee, used both the hot and cold baths and enjoyed massages. The Roman citizen devoted a large part of his time to *otium*,

Cold water pool (*frigidarium*) in the Forum Baths, about 120 BC, Pompeii.

that is this kind of relaxation and activities outside his working life (*negotium*).

The oldest baths in Pompeii are the '*terme stabiane*', dating to the Samnite period and reconstructed on various occasions. The central area was taken up with a large courtyard, with a *palaestra*, an open area for taking exercise before the bath, flanked on one side by a swimming pool and changing cubicles. On the other were the baths proper, one reserved for men and the other for women. Here there were also changing cubicles for men and women, the *tepidarium* (with pools containing warm water) and *calidarium* (with hot water pools), while the space with the cold pool (*frigidarium*) was only to be found in the men's section. The whole area was richly decorated in painting and plaster work with mosaic pavements, statues and fountains.

The baths in the Forum are

View of the *palaestra* in the Stabian baths, about 150 BC. Pompeii. The large courtyard used as the *palaestra* or exercise ground, was flanked by pools and changing rooms.

smaller but also beautifully decorated. The *frigidarium* is particularly interesting, in a splendid round chamber with four side niches: at the centre was the large circular marble bath surmounted by a cupola.

The *tepidarium* was covered in white plaster decoration with niches framed by *telamones* (statues of human figures) appearing to hold up the vaulted ceiling. These baths were fed by a sophisticated plumbing system using the very latest technology.

Physical excellence was also pursued in the large *palaestra*, surrounded by a high wall, with a portico and internal pool. Many bodies were discovered in the area of the exercise grounds, trapped no doubt as they tried to escape at the time of the eruption.

Wall painting with architectural motifs, from the Villa of the Mysteries, one of the most interesting examples of painting in the Pompeii Second Style.

The wall painting discovered at Pompeii offers a rare and detailed insight into an art form otherwise almost totally destroyed. Pompeii provides a survey of wall painting over a century and a half under the Romans until the time of the eruption in 79 AD.

The paintings can be divided stylistically into four periods. The First or 'Masonry' Style, well established by the 2nd century BC, features stucco

Wall paintings
in the House
of the Faun,
about 120 BC.

Peristyle and garden of the House of the Vettii.

The House of the Vettii

The House of the Vettii has a large atrium in the Tuscanic style opening directly on to the rectangular peristyle.

There appears to have been no *tablinum,* the space reserved for welcoming guests. In the *tricliniium* an elaborate frieze decoration with cupids was discovered all along the wall.

The house belonged to rich merchants and gives us a good idea of the lifestyle of the more affluent classes in Pompeii in the 1ˢᵗ century AD The paintings date to the period of reconstruction following the earthquake of 62 AD.

The garden here has recently been replanted in an attempt to recreate its classical appearance: the plants were chosen after studying the carbonized roots in the soil below the ash.

painted in imitation of precious marble and alabaster. This style, widely diffused in the Hellenistic world, can be seen in the decoration of the House of the Faun in Pompeii.

The Second or 'Architectural' Style, dating to the 1ˢᵗ century BC, incorporates elaborate architectural views inspired by theatrical sets. An outstanding example of this is in the Villa of the Mysteries in Pompeii and in the Villa at Boscoreale.

The Third Style, popular from the middle of the 1ˢᵗ century BC to the middle of the 1ˢᵗ century AD is characterized by polychrome decoration. There is extraordinary attention to detail and often painting of remarkable elegance.

In the centre of the wall a scene, usually of narrative or mythological subject matter, was often a copy or inspired by a Greek original. This Third

Style is evident in some homes such as the House of Lucretius Fronto, with paintings showing the *Death of Neoptolemus* and *Venus and Mars* or the home of Cecilius Giocondus, with a scene of *Iphigenia in Taurus.* The Last or Fourth Style, in vogue from the last 25 years or so of Pompeii's existence, saw the return of architectural elements, but used in fantastical contexts, without any respect for realism or the conventional architectural 'orders', with some areas worked in stucco relief: for example the House of the Vettii and of the Lovers in Pompeii and Nero's *Domus Aurea* in Rome.

Many of the finest wall paintings from Pompeii are now kept for the sake of conservation in the National Archaeological Museum in Naples.

Iphigenia in Taurus. National Archaeological Museum, Naples. Wall paintings featuring a narrative or mythological scene are typical of Pompeii's Third Style.

The Mosaics

Pompeii provides a rich sample of the range of mosaics found throughout the Roman world.

Mosaic work first appeared in Republican Rome, imported from Greece, and developed fully in the first years of the Empire. It was used above all in pavement decoration but was sometimes extended to cover the surface of walls, as in the decoration of the fountain in the House of the Bear in Pompeii, although very few examples of this survive. Various techniques were involved in mosaic work.

The earliest mosaics were made with terracotta pieces, later replaced by squares of marble or stone: the black and white *tassellati*. Some two centuries later tiles (*crustae*) in a variety of colours and sizes cut into geometrical or floral patterns appeared.

This kind of inlay marble decoration was well adapted to covering large surfaces. Even livelier depictions could be created with mosaic

Detail of Alexander the Great from the mosaic of the *Battle of Issus*, late 2nd century BC. This large polychrome mosaic comes from the House of the Faun in Pompeii and is now at the National Archaeological Museum in Naples.

The House of the Faun

In the western part of Pompeii, not far from the Forum, is the House of the Faun, which takes its name from the statuette of a dancing faun originally decorating the pool of the *impluvium* and now in the National Archaeological Museum in Naples. The house, probably begun in the Samnite period, has two atriums and two peristyles, one with a fountain at the centre, the other with a garden and Doric portico. One of the most beautiful mosaics of the world of antiquity, a magnificent representation of the battle of Alexander the Great at Issus, came from a room here. The room had a colonnaded front opening onto the larger peristyle and was set between two rooms used as summer dining rooms. The battle scene was probably taken from the original work of a great Greek painter. The mosaic is in *opus vermiculatum*, with about one million *tesserae* packed densely together.

vermiculatum used to create paintings in marble. This involved quite minute pieces that allowed for the gradual shading of colour and for the different effects created by vitreous and stone tiles. In addition to single figures and small scenes large paintings such as the depiction of the battle of Battle of Issus in the House of the Faun were also reproduced in mosaic. A variety of subjects are depicted in the mosaics in Pompeii, mostly now conserved in the National Archaeological Museum in Naples: from simple geometrical motifs to large and complex scenes, watchdogs guarding the entrance, or scenes of combat as in the mosaic from the *palaestra*.

Mosaic pavement from the reception room (*tablinum*) of the House of Paquius Proculus, Pompeii. The decoration has small framed images of animals.

Opposite: Mosaic with warning *cave canem* or 'beware of the dog', from Pompeii's House of the Tragic Poet, 1st century AD.

Mosaic with fish, National Archaeological Museum, Naples. The *tesserae* are arranged to convey minute detail and lighting effects.

SCULPTURE

Statues, found in the villas and more opulent houses of Pompeii, performed both a decorative and a symbolic role.

In private houses sculptured portraits were of great importance: in the atrium where the host welcomed his guests the shrine to the house gods included portraits of the family's ancestors or, if the proprietor were a freedman (an ex-slave who had become rich or acquired respectable status), statues of his previous owners. As far as garden statuary was concerned subjects were usually linked to the theme of Dionysus. A wealth of fountain sculpture survives, for the most part associated with stories related to water.

The production of sculpture in Pompeii, as in the whole Roman world, is heavily indebted to Greek models largely brought to Italy as plunder and is for the most part based on copies of classical and Hellenistic originals.

Statue of a dancing faun, about 120 BC, which gives its name to the House of the Faun in Pompeii. Many statues from fountains and gardens are associated with the cult of Dionysius.

Temple for the household gods at the House of Menander, Pompeii, where portraits of ancestors would have been displayed.

Portraits of ancestors in the atrium of the Roman house

Ancestor worship was of fundamental importance to Roman civilization, especially in patrician families. Polybius, the Greek historian who lived in Rome in the 2nd century BC, accurately describes homage paid to the illustrious dead. After the funeral it was customary to display an image of the deceased, an accurate likeness in wax, in the most prominent position in the house, enclosed within a wooden tabernacle. This image was an object of great veneration and was made part of any solemn sacrifice or public ceremony.

The images of ancestors were displayed in the funeral processions of other family members. Veneration of ancestors glorified the patrician family who were granted the legal privilege of housing these images in the atrium, the focus of the home: this law, the *ius imaginum*, exemplifies the social importance attached to the conservation of these images.

Economic Life: Agriculture and Livestock

Wall painting from the House of the Vettii, Pompeii, showing *putti* transporting grapes. Wine production was one of the main activities at the Roman villas in the countryside around Pompeii.

The Roman world, and the world of antiquity in general, based its economy on agriculture: agricultural production ensured the success of a number of other activities such as crafts and trade. The Roman aristocracy and affluent classes invested a large part of their wealth in agriculture.

The rich chose to live in the most productive zones where they built villas that also served as working and highly organised farms. Farm labour and other activities related to agricultural production was

mostly carried out by slaves.

Even though free labourers existed the success on any enterprise depended on a large slave workforce. Food was processed and stored in the part of the villa known as the *pars rustica*. The proprietor, the *dominus*, had a residential area of the villa separate from the working farm where he was able to enjoy all the pleasures of country life. This was a great advantage as the Romans, like ourselves, had complaints about the chaos and noise of city life. The *pars rustica* also housed livestock: there were stables and pigsties as well as pens and enclosures for poultry. There was no wastage with the animals: they were used for meat, wool and their skins, for milk and eggs, for transport and for work in the fields. Beekeeping was of paramount

Wall painting with a rabbit and figs. National Archaeological Museum, Naples. The farm estates of Roman villas produced a rich variety of livestock and produce.

Opposite: Mosaic with three villa buildings, trees and vines, from Tabarka, 3rd-4th century AD. Bardo Museum, Tunis.

importance for wax and particularly for honey, as this was the only natural sweetener then available. A villa could produce its own meat, vegetables, grain, eggs, milk and honey. Together with the vegetable gardens

there were orchards for fruit production: paintings from Pompeii offer an insight into fertile gardens with flowers growing among bushes and below laden fruit trees.

Wall painting with a cock and hen. National Archaeological Museum, Naples

Oil and Wine: from Production to Sale and Consumption

The cultivation of vines and olives was vital to the Roman economy and was a main feature of life at the villa. In the *pars rustica* there was an olive press, together with devices for squashing the grapes. Although most of the agricultural production was designed to make the villa self sufficient any surplus could be sold. Olive oil was used for cooking and for beauty products while wine

was drunk liberally by all social classes. It had been produced in the eastern Mediterranean for centuries and was introduced to Rome by Greek settlers in southern Italy. Production became both specialised and diversified and the Roman world had access to an extraordinary range of wines. A huge quantity of amphorae, the containers most suited to transporting liquids, was uncovered in the excavations of Pompeii and from the bottom of the sea from wrecked trading vessels.

The success of the wine trade in the Roman world is reflected in the enormous number of these amphorae found in the whole Mediterranean basin.

Relief showing grapes being pressed. Archaeological Museum, Venice.

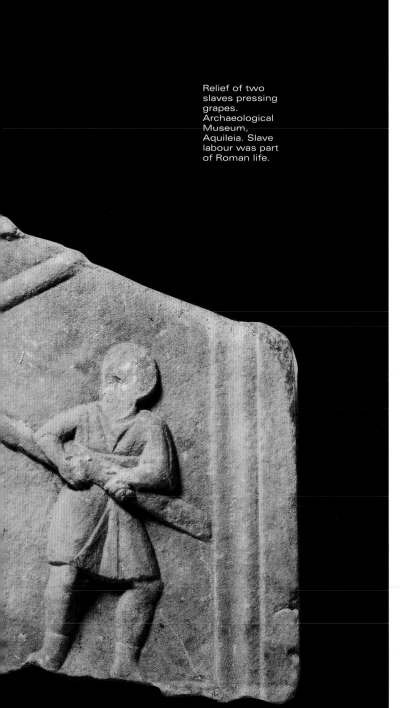

Relief of two
slaves pressing
grapes.
Archaeological
Museum,
Aquileia. Slave
labour was part
of Roman life.

Slaves

The success of Roman
agricultural operations,
especially when based on
the villa of a rich landowner,
depended on slavery. The
heavy slave workforce
cut production costs as
slaves were given only the
sustenance required to keep
them alive and healthy.

Slaves were considered
as commodities. They were
usually set limited tasks in
which they could become
proficient such as ploughing,
sowing or pruning.

There were also slaves in
charge of breeding livestock,
and others who milked the
cows and made cheese. Olive
production and grape pressing
were also handled by slaves.

As the villa was so
dependent on this workforce
slaves tended to be treated
well, but never with
extravagance. It was in the
landlord's interest to keep
them healthy and not to
subject them to danger.

They were paid in grain,

with the amount varying in accordance with the task performed: those doing heavy physical work received more than those with less exhausting occupations.

The reliance on slave labour certainly contributed to the lack of technological progress in the Roman world. It was not the lack of understanding or technological capability which prevented progress on this front, but rather the absence of any need to invest in alternative systems when slave power worked so well.

The slave, both man and tool, was highly efficient, reliable, cost effective, loyal and therefore preferable to any other solution.

Mosaic with a banquet scene, from Carthage, 3rd-4th century AD. Bardo Museum, Tunis. In the centre a figure carries a basket on his head.

Mosaic with
labourers,
3rd-4th century AD.
Bardo Museum,
Tunis.

Arts and Crafts

Craftsmen provided goods essential to the efficient working of the Empire.

There was a marked increase in the number of artisans' shops from the 2nd century BC, following Rome's Mediterranean expansion and the resulting increase in prosperity.

Many craftsmen and artisans worked independently in small shops where they both produced and sold their goods; others were salaried workers in larger enterprises which also took on slaves.

They produced everyday objects such as kitchen equipment, furniture, material and clothing, lamps, footwear, barrels, amphorae, jars and a range of other goods essential to everyday life in trade, transport and the building sectors.

The location of these workshops and their situation was very important as, for example, metal workers and potters needed ovens and furnaces which reached very high temperatures. These were a danger to the urban community and the fumes they created also posed a threat. Metal workers and potters were usually therefore found on the city's outskirts or in sparsely populated areas.

Stonemasons, carpenters and other craftsmen who did not use dangerous equipment had workshops on the ground floor of an *insula*, preferably on a busy thoroughfare.

An important element of urban life, especially in the Imperial age, was played by the *collegia*, a sort of trade union, bringing together workers in order to protect their interests. The most widespread unions were those of the builders, weavers, tailors, merchants, carpenters and bakers.

Each union had its own statute, headquarters, flag, chosen deity, and funds raised from the contributions of its members. The archaeological evidence from Pompeii

Fragment of a memorial plaque or *stele* dedicated to a carpenter. Archaeological Museum, Aquileia. A number of these are carved with the tools of the craftsman's trade.

reflects the significance of these associations: the unions took an active part in electoral campaigns for the renewal of city and provincial magistrates.

One of the campaign notices put up by the union of fullers recommends a candidate for his honesty, generosity and administrative acumen.

A bakery in Pompeii

There are enough bakeries and pastry shops in Pompeii to suggest that they were commonly found across the city. Bakers ground the grain to make flour before baking the bread and selling it.
In a bakery in an old part of the city, in the Vicolo Storto, 80 burnt round and elongated rolls were found in the oven.

Not far-from the oven were a number of large black millstones of volcanic rock, used to grind the grain. These were erected on to bases built of mortar. Containers of water nearby suggest that it was also used during bread production, probably to obtain a cranckling crust.

Graffiti in Pompeii with electoral messages from the 1ˢᵗ century AD.

The craftsman united into guilds were actively involved in election campaigning.

Memorial plaque or stele showing a blacksmith's forge. Archaeological Museum, Aquileia.

Flourishing Commercial Activity

Opposite:
Wall painting
showing the
port of a city
in Campania,
1st century AD.
National
Archaeological
Museum,
Naples.

Relief of
a cloth
merchant.
Uffizi Gallery,
Florence.
Cloth was
an important
part of the
commercial life
of the time.

The development of
commercial activity in the
Roman world is linked to
the expansion and control
of maritime trade routes,
combined with the complex
and efficient road network
connecting all the ports and
major trading centres.

Agriculture and livestock

were the basis of the
earliest trading operations
but as Rome gradually
strengthened its hold over the
Mediterranean it became the
centre of a diversified market
handling any variety of goods.

Archaeological finds
recovered from sunken
Roman ships bear witness
both to the volume of traffic
and to the wide range of
goods transported.

Together with grain and
other food products, trade
grew to include linen and
Egyptian papyrus; marble,
pottery and honey from
Greece; perfumes, spices,
and purple dye from Syria and
Phoenicia; skins, salt, horses
and slaves from Germany,
Pannonia and Dacia; wine,
oil and cloth from Spain and
Gaul; and wild animals and
ivory from Asia and Africa.
There were many opportunities
for an adventurous trader
to increase his wealth.

Although the market

appeared to be dominated
by imports, certain Italian
products were always highly
prized abroad, such as pots
and metalwork from Arezzo
and Campania, wine and oil
from central and southern Italy,
and cloth from northern Italy.

Trading by sea was most
widely used, as the overland
routes were slower and
therefore more expensive.

Although the economy in
the Roman period preserved
many of the traits of
antiquity, paying little heed
to the laws of supply and
demand which regulate our
markets, there are many
indications of the emergence
of something approaching
a modern economy: for
example the flourishing of
commercial enterprise, the
wealth it produced, the
possibility of investment
options, and the creation
of interest-based loans.

Detail from
the relief of a
cloth merchant,
Uffizi Gallery,
Florence.

The Romans devoted a
great deal of attention to the
kitchen and to meals. Among
the typical dishes *puls* was
a staple: a porridge mixture
made of a number of cereals,
flavoured with herbs such as
oregano and mint and dressed
with oil. Goats' cheeses and
vegetables were served to give
variety to this simple dish.

The most common
vegetables were chicory,
turnips, cabbages, leeks, edible
wild plants and asparagus.

The Romans enjoyed fruit,
home-grown as well as the
more exotic produce of the
Orient: apples, pears and
imported cherries were eaten
together with figs, walnuts,
almonds, chestnuts, as well
as dates and apricots from
Africa and Asia Minor.

There were various types
of bread: the *panis candidus*,
from the finest and most
expensive white flour, *panis*

Ruins of a
bakery of the
1st century AD,
Pompeii.

secundarius, second best as its name makes clear, and bread made from bran (*plebeius*), which even the very poor could afford.

According to Pliny, the first bakeries only appeared after 171 BC, before when bread was only made in the home. Meat was only usually eaten on special occasions, although the rich enjoyed it more frequently: roast or boiled, it was flavoured with spices and sauces.

A sauce called *garum* was popular. It was made with fish and its quality varied according to the type and freshness of the fish used: tuna and mackerel were used for the most delicate flavour; anchovies for the *garum* of

the poor and servants. Various farmyard animals were used as meat, with pork and poultry being widely consumed; hens were only eaten when they could no longer produce eggs.

Cattle were highly prized for work in the fields: slaughtering these animals was considered a crime of the same gravity as killing a slave, also considered an agricultural tool.

Game was the key ingredient at the most prestigious banquets: wild boar, deer, stag, thrushes, partridge, but also starling and quail. Fish was available to those who could afford it, especially shellfish and mussels. Water and milk were drunk and of course wine, not usually consumed straight but watered down.

Still-life with grapes and game, 1st century AD. National Archaeological Museum, Naples. Rich Romans enjoyed a very varied diet.

The Banquet of Trimalchio, narrated by Petronius

In his *Satyricon* Petronius describes a lavish banquet given by the nouveau-riche Trimalchio to his friends. The courses are interspersed with a series of dialogues, jokes, jests and above all a range of special effects linked to the presentation of the food. A pig is served whole and while the owner of the house pretends to berate the servant for having forgotten to gut it the servant grabs a knife and cuts open the animal to reveal the sausages and black puddings.

The greatest coup was kept until the end of the feast when a dish was brought in full of special breads, with a giant Priapus in the middle made of pastry and stuffed with every kind of fruit. When the breads were touched, to everybody's delight, a shower of saffron burst out: a spice used in cults and sacred ritual. After the special bread *focacce*, fruit was eaten. One of the guests recounts *'there followed such gluttonous consumption that the very memory of it fills me with disgust. Instead of thrushes large hens were brought in, one for each guest, accompanied by hooded goose eggs. Trimalchio insisted that we eat the chickens, saying that they had been boned'*.

The Banquet: a Social Festivity

The banquet, the ancient *symposium* derived from the Greeks, was introduced to Italy at the time of the Etruscans, when the close relations between the Etruscans and the Italic peoples with the colonial Greeks spread the practice of this particular way of enjoying food and drink.

Whether in his country villa or at home in the city the wealthy Roman loved to surround himself with friends and hold a banquet in the *triclinium*. Three couches arranged around a low table provided the basic furnishing for a banquet: the fourth side was left free to allow the slaves to come and go with the various courses: the food was rich and varied.

The dessert was usually fruit, possibly of the more exotic kind: dates, sultanas and raisins, Syrian pears, pomegranates, figs and cherries imported from the Orient. Sweets were only made for the most extravagant banquets such as the one described in the *Satyricon* by Petronius.

Wine was consumed with the meal, and after the main dishes, when the fruit and sweets were served, a mixture of honey and wine was offered. This signalled a series of toasts and libations, often accompanied by lewd jokes, songs, dancing, musical performances and acting: entertainments often lasted throughout the night.

Wall painting of a banquet scene. National Archaeological Museum, Naples.

Relief showing
men buying
meat in a
shop. Ostiense
Museum, Ostia.

Medicine and Health

Health was clearly closely associated with diet. Seneca in his *Letters* describes the catastrophic effects of over-eating, including obesity, gallstones and gout, but makes no mention of the health hazards related to malnutrition and sanitary problems which affected the very poor.

Social and economic conditions certainly determined the quality of life and longevity. The higher social classes generally lived longer, despite the 'illnesses induced by luxury' so decried by Seneca. Infections of the respiratory system, just to cite one example, were a plague on the lower orders of society as they lived in unhealthy and overcrowded conditions. Their houses were lacking in air and light and had no water or sanitation.

Death in childbirth was frequent, as was infant mortality, but this was common to all societies before the advent of modern medicine.

The Romans did attempt to safeguard the health of the people with a number of regulations. Under the Republic a political office was founded to control the quality of food put on the market. Doctors did not appear in Rome until much later: citizens interested in preserving their health turned rather to the goddesses Salus and Febris with their prayers. The god Aesclepius (taken over from the Greek god

Opposite:
Bust of Seneca from the Baroque period. Rubens' House, Antwerp. In his *Letters* Seneca describes a number of illnesses and health problems associated with over-eating.

Roman doctor's case. National Archaeological Museum, Naples.

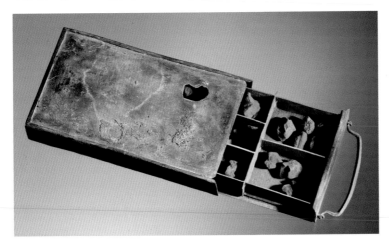

of medicine) entered the Roman pantheon in the 3rd century *pantheon* BC.

The first doctors to appear were of Greek-Hellenistic origin. They were originally given little respect, as many of them were slaves captured during the Roman campaigns.

These Greek doctors were the first to open pharmacies or *tabernae medicorum,* which also served as first-aid posts and schools for training followers. But it was only in 77 BC with the arrival in Rome from Bithynia of the doctor and teacher Asclepiades that medicine began to be considered a scientific discipline.

In 10 AD Augustus allowed doctors to form associations which helped promote some sort of public health system. The most famous doctor in the Roman period was Galen of Pergamo, personal doctor to the emperor Marcus Aurelius: his famous book the *Ars Medica,* was the standard medical text until the 17th century.

Wall painting of a centaur between Apollo and Aesculapius. National Archaeological Museum, Naples. Aesculapius is the Roman god of medicine, his name derived from the Greek Asclepio.

The Role of Women in Marriage and the Family

Women played an influential role in private and public life in Rome. Unmarried girls in Pompeii, like those in Rome, led fairly secluded lives but acquired greater freedom when married. Roman matrons, unlike their Greek counterparts, were not obliged to stay indoors but went out to shop and see their friends and attended banquets with their husbands. Marriages were arranged by parents.

Girls as young as 12 or 13 were considered old enough to marry, as were boys at 14, although it was rare for boys to marry so early. There were at least two types of marriage contract: the *conventio in manum* and the *matrimonio sine manu* or unrestricted contract.

With the first and most ancient the woman became a 'matron': she became a member of her husband's family and subject to the authority or *patria potestas* of her father-in-law, like any of his other daughters.

This type of marriage entailed a number of rituals,

Wall painting from the Villa of the Mysteries showing a bride at her toilette, about 50 BC.

including the *confarreatio,* which took its name form the bread of spelt wheat (*farrum*) divided by the couple, and the *coemptio*, the sale, at first real but then only symbolic, of the bride by her father to the new husband.

With a marriage *sine manu,* the bride remained under the authority or *patria potestas* of her own father and therefore tied to her family of origin.

This type of contract was far less binding than the first and could be dissolved by the agreed separation of the couple. It became increasingly popular from the last days of the Republic. In the less formal marriage based on *usus* the man and woman had only to live together for a year.

Apart from the *usus* contract, which only entailed the bride moving into the house of the groom, or vice versa, and was celebrated if at all with a banquet, the other contracts were accompanied by traditional rituals and ceremonies.

The bride wore a white tunic drawn in at the waist with a belt and covered her head with a red veil. She left her childhood home in order to hear the wedding contract read out in front of witnesses. Once

the practical and economic preliminaries were over the real ceremony began.

The *pronuba*, a matron and friend of the family who had still to be married to her first husband, had the role of holding the right hands of the bride and groom together, to symbolize their union as man and wife.

Following the traditional banquet and final toasts the marriage procession was led by the bride and three children: two walked at either side and one ahead of her carrying a flaming torch from the bride's house. The bride herself carried a spindle and was followed by all the guests.

When she reached her husband's house the door was opened and the bride performed a propitiatory act by decorating the entrance with strips of wool coated in scented pig fat.

The groom who reached the house before her asks her name to receive the formulaic response: '*Ubi tu Gaius, ego Gaia*'. He then lifted her up into his arms and carried her over the threshold.

Wall painting showing the dressing of the bride. National Archaeological Museum, Naples. The marriage ritual began with a bath and the preparation of the bride.

Fashion, Dress and Make-up

In the Roman world, men and women wore a tunic drawn in at the waist and made of two rectangles of wool, linen and cotton sewn together along the sides leaving a hole for the head and arms.

It had no sleeves but the arms are partially covered by the folds of material falling off the shoulder. A wide vertical purple band (*latus clavius*) indicated senatorial rank on a man's tunic.

A toga was worn over the man's tunic, a *stola* over the woman's. The white woollen toga was wrapped around the body and secured on the left shoulder from where it is passed under the right arm and returned to hang over the left arm. Magistrates and some senators wore a white toga with a purple border (*toga praetexta*). Children too wore a *praetexta* as a sign of the almost priestly respect due to them. At the age of 17 a solemn ceremony marked their passage into maturity when they began to wear *toga pura* or *virilis*, white and without any decoration.

The *stola* was a floor-length garment sewn with a number of pleats and drawn in at the waist with a belt, occasionally with a second belt or band worn below the breast. It might have two sleeves, no sleeves or just a sleeve on one side.

A rectangular cloak was also worn in winter, knotted at the front around the neck, and worn with or without a hood. Sandals were worn in the home, but open and laced bootlets (*calcei*) were preferred outdoors.

Men nearly always wore their hair cut short in very simple styles. Women's hair was loose until they were married and was then plaited and wrapped around the head. In the Imperial age women's hair fashions became more extravagant and wigs and

Barberini Statue, of a figure in a toga with busts of his ancestors, 1ˢᵗ century BC. Palace of the Conservatori, Rome. The toga was the traditional dress of men in ancient Rome.

Wall painting of a girl pouring perfume. National Archaeological Museum, Rome. The Romans constantly used scented essences and oils for personal hygiene, ceremonial and ritual purposes, at banquets and during theatrical performances.

hairpieces were used. Hair removal came into vogue as did the more widespread use of perfumes and creams.

Men were nearly always clean-shaven and beards were rare until the late Imperial period when they became more popular. Jewellery was inspired by Etruscan, Greek and Oriental designs until the end of the 1st century BC, when the first school for Roman goldsmiths opened.

Perfume was an essential ingredient of public and private life in Rome: in the theatre the audience was showered with essences from the *velaria*; during banquets doves might be released, their wings soaked in perfume, while the guests, already well perfumed on arrival, washed their hands in aromatic waters between each course. Perfumes were also burnt during funeral rituals and the groom would cover the doorway of his bride's house with perfume of the day of the wedding.

Perfume making was one of the most highly paid professions in Rome: *unguentarii* (or *myrobecharii*) produced and sold the concoctions made in their own workshops.

Perfumes were made from flowers, bushes, roots and the rest of the plants, either by pressing or by leaving them to soak in fats, before heating to extract the essential oils.

The essence was then added to liquid made of unripe olive oil (for ointments) or from sour grapes (for perfumes).

Bust of a woman, from the Tomb of the Haterii, 100 AD. Vatican Palace, Rome. The woman hair's hair is dressed in the elaborate style of the period.

School and Education

Holding high public office was inconceivable in ancient Rome without the benefit of a long and costly education.

Small abacus, used by school children for doing sums. National Archaeological Museum, Rome.

The first paying 'school', according to Plutarch, was set up in Rome by a freedman, the grammarian Spurius Carvilius, at the end of the 3rd century BC. Before then the child's education was entrusted to the family. From birth to the age of seven, a boy was left in the care of his mother and nurse, after which he was passed on to his father who taught him to read and write together with basic arithmetic, or personally oversaw lessons given by a tutor.

The most highly regarded tutors were writers, poets and scholars, originally from Magna Grecia, and often men who had been taken as slaves, like Livius Andronicus from Taranto.

Only the richest families could afford to employ a resident tutor: others had to rely on improvised schools set up by a master who took in small groups of boys for a small fee.

Schools gradually became more popular. They were financed by parents and run, according to the level, by a *litterator* at the elementary stage, with children from 7 to 11 (*ludus litterarius*); by a *grammaticus* in the middle school, catering for 12 to 17 year olds (*grammatici schola*), and by a *rhetor* at the highest level the *rhetoris schola* where young men could stay on until they were 20. Elementary schools were mixed while the middle and upper schools were almost exclusively for boys.

An elementary school teacher in the Republican period was considered one of the lowest professions and the object of fierce satire.

Grammarians and rhetoricians also received minimal wages. Higher education was open to a select few and those who pursued it were destined to become part of the political and cultural elite in Rome.

A *grammaticus* guided boys through secondary education with the study of grammar (phoenetics, morphology and syntax), Greek culture, history, geography, astronomy and physics, combined to form the liberal arts. Greek and Latin literature were also part of the curriculum.

A young aristocrat's education would have been thought complete when he had mastered oratory, taught by a specialised *rhetor* or *orator*, who passed on the stylistic rules essential to solemn and elevated discourse and above all to public speaking.

It was mastering rhetoric that ensured a successful life in politics and the public arena.

Writing equipment, 1st-2nd century AD, British Museum, London.

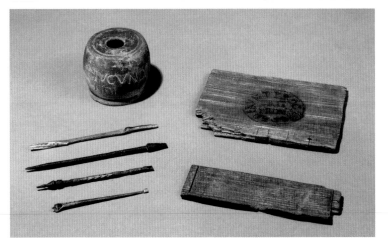

Painting from
Pompeii of a
portrait of a boy
with a laurel
crown. National
Archaeological
Museum,
Naples. Only
a restricted
circle of young
Romans
enjoyed any
form of higher
education.

Popular Entertainment: Games and Spectacles

The Romans thrived on spectacle: chariot races, musical and theatrical performances, gladiatorial combat, hunts and sea battles.

All were accompanied by formal rituals and held in appropriately designed spaces.

There was a clear distintion between *ludi* and *munera*. The first and oldest were the *ludi* or games in celebration of a particular deity: they were mainly chariot races and elaborate spectacles.

The second (from *munus*,

Bas-relief with scenes from the comic theatre, 1st century AD. National Archaeological Museum, Naples.

Relief with circus games, from Pompeii. National Archaeological Museum, Naples. Chariot races and contests between gladiators and wild beasts took place in the amphitheatre.

gift) were offered to the people by the organizers. They could be either public or private and included games in the amphitheatre.

The citizens did not usually take an active part in the games: the lower orders and even slaves were the main participants.

The magistrates involved in the organization of the games were conscious that their success was a vital way of winning popular support. In the Imperial age the games were manipulated by the emperors themselves and used for propaganda.

The expression 'panem

et circenses' – bread and circuses – indicated all that was needed to gain the favour of the masses: the distribution of grain satisfied their hunger while the games and spectacles kept them entertained.

A number of writers and intellectuals criticised in biting satires the gradual degeneration of the masses. In the days of the Republic they had taken part in the life of the state and shown an interest in politics, but under the Empire they had become duped into asking for nothing more than to have their stomachs filled and to be entertained.

Following pages: Mosaic with circus scenes, now in the Borghese Gallery, Rome. Many gladiators became popular heroes.

Detail of a gladiator from the mosaic of circus scenes, Borghese Gallery, Rome.

Gladiatorial Combat

Gladiatorial combat was one of the most popular spectacles in the amphitheatre. Gladiators were trained in special schools.

The most famous were in Campania, such as the one at Capua. The men were usually slaves whose names reflected their place of origin, like the Dalmatians and the Thracians. But there were also freemen, voluntary professionals attracted by the rewards and the chance to win fame and glory.

The combat was to the death and the crowd enjoyed the spilling of blood. It might also decide to spare an exhausted combatant and when one fell to the ground would shout either 'mitte!' (save him!) or 'jugula!' (do him in!).

The games in the arena generally lasted a whole day.

They were dominated by chariot races, proceeded by a splendid procession (pompa) headed by the magistrate and the sponsor of the games, followed by all the participants accompanied by musicians, notably trumpet and horn players.

In the chariot races the driver, dressed in a short tunic in the colour of his team and with his head protected by a helmet, stood erect on the light wooden structure.

The reins were tied to his chest and guided by the left hand while in the right he held the crop to urge the horses on. The course was run numerous times so that each charioteer would cover a number of kilometres.

Accidents were frequent, often provoked by foul play. Horses, chariot and driver were frequently upturned with disastrous consequences in risky overtaking manoeuvres.

Relief of a chariot race, 1st-2nd century AD, British Museum, London. These races were very popular: the charioteers ran tremendous risks in dangerous competitions.

ANNIAE
ARESCVSA

Wall painting
of a chariot
race. National
Archaeological
Museum,
Naples.

Relief showing
a chariot race.
Archaeological
Museum,
Foligno. Scenes
like this convey

something of
the danger and
excitement of
these highly
popular events.

The Roman pantheon grew to absorb Italic deities and other foreign imports especially Greek ones.

Jupiter was the most important of those within the 'Capitoline Trinity', the main gods of Rome, a position he shared with Juno and Minerva.

All the heavenly signs were attributes of Jupiter, the god of lightning and rain. He protected marriage vows and all sacred contracts. His wife Juno, an ancient Italic goddess, was later identified with the Greek goddess Hera, the wife of Zeus. She was the goddess of the Moon and consecrated to the night, patron of marriage and of the family. As such she was hostile to public prostitutes.

Another goddess of Italic origin was Minerva whose cult was introduced to Rome in the 4th century BC. She was the patron of intellectual activity, of the arts and crafts, of inventiveness and wisdom. Mars, an ancient divinity of the Latini, was originally the god of arable and animal farming.

He was promoted to the god of war when the Roman world's expansion by conquest began to overshadow primarily agricultural activities. March, the month when military expeditions were organized, was dedicated to Mars.

Diana, the virgin goddess of the woods and of the hunt, was identified with the Greek goddess Artemis. She also had a celestial aspect, making her a rival of Juno, as she too was associated with the moon and with childbirth.

Venus, the Roman equivalent to the Greek Aphrodite, was the goddess of beauty, love, the fertility of Spring and as such the patron of gardens.

From the time of Julius Caesar, whose family,

Statue of seated
Jupiter, Vatican
Palace, Rome.
Jupiter was
the main god
of the Roman
pantheon.

Wall painting
from Pompeii
showing Venus
and Mars,
the gods of
Love and War
respectively.
National
Archaeological
Museum,
Naples.

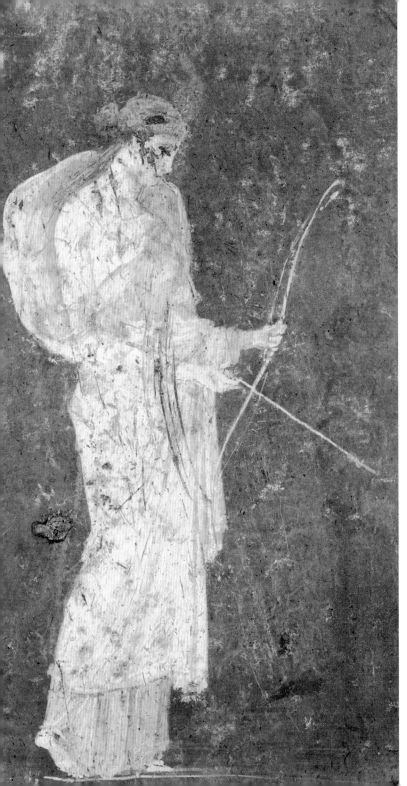

through Aeneas claimed to be descended from Venus herself, the cult to Venus genitrix (the giver of life) gained hold. Together with Mars, from whom Romulus was descended, they formed a new couple in the official religion of the Empire.

Venus and Mars were the parents of Eros, who represented amorous desire, while Priapus, who symbolized natural strength and the sexual impulse, was thought to be the offspring of Venus and Dionysus.

Among the typically Roman deities was Vesta, an ancient goddess associated with the domestic and public hearth, and Fortune, venerated as *Fors Fortuna*, in recognition of the supreme importance played by chance.

Wall painting of Diana, goddess of the hunt and woods. National Archaeological Museum, Naples.

The Capitoline Trinity

The three main gods of the Roman pantheon, Jupiter, Juno and Minerva, or the 'Capitoline Trinity', were so called because of the temple dedicated to them on the Capitol in Rome. Originally the trinity was composed of Jupiter, Mars and Quirino, with Jupiter as protector of the state and Mars and Quirino as gods of war: eventually Mars and Quirino were replaced by Juno and Minerva. In the forum in Pompeii there was also a temple dedicated to the trinity called the *Capitolium*. The monumental head of Jupiter came from this site: the statue was made to be supported by a wooden structure. Only the head and extremities were of marble while the rest of the body, draped in cloth, was made of wood.

Relief of Marcus Aurelius performing a sacrifice; in the background is a temple on the Capitol Hill dedicated to Jupiter. Capitoline Museum, Rome.

Pompeii: a City Dedicated to Venus

Venus, as patron goddess of the city, enjoyed a flourishing cult in Pompeii. When the city became a Roman colony, it was called *Colonia Veneria Cornelia Pompeiianorum*, in honour of Lucius Cornelius Sulla, the general who conquered Pompeii, and Venus, the patron goddess of the city.

The temple of Venus Pompeiiana was the most important in the city. It was built under the Samnites and later enlarged and covered in precious marbles. It was undergoing improvements in 79 AD at the time of the eruption. Had the temple, with its majestic porticoes, been finished it would have been the most monumental in Pompeii.

The numerous statues and paintings of Venus found in the houses of the city bear witness to the strength of her cult. In a painted scene in the peristyle of the House of Venus, for example, she is shown on a large shell against the blue of the sea.

In one hand she holds a veil swollen by the breeze, her hair is elaborately dressed but she wears nothing but her jewels: a crown, necklace, bracelets and ankle bands.

Two cupids flank the shell, one riding a dolphin.

Pompeii's Temple of Venus, the patron goddess of the city, 1st century BC - 1st century AD.

Detail from
the statue of
Venus, in the
Antiquarium,
Pompeii.

Wall painting from the House of Venus in Pompeii, showing Venus rising from the sea escorted by putti.

The Cult of Apollo

The cult of Apollo in Pompeii
has very ancient origins:
fragments of inscriptions in
Etruscan with dedications
to Apollo have been dated
to the 6th century BC.

A temple surrounded by
a portico on all four sides
was built in the 2nd century
BC. The *cella*, facing south,
was raised on a platform
with columns on each side
while the pavement was
decorated with mosaics.

After the 62 AD earthquake
restoration began on the
temple: the structure was
to be partially covered in
coloured stucco. A statue
of Apollo and a bust of his
sister Artemis, originally
in the temple, are now in
the National Archaeological
Museum of Naples, with
copies in Pompeii. His
effigy was also found in
private houses, such as
the one in the home of
Julius Polibius, bearing
witness to the importance
of his cult in the city.

View of the
temple of
Apollo, 2nd
century BC,
Pompeii. The
cult of Apollo
in Pompeii dates
from the 6th
century BC.

Mystery Cults and Oriental Divinities

At the time of the Republic, although it was not forbidden to practise foreign religions in Rome, imported deities enjoyed no official recognition: this situation remained virtually unchanged in the first 200 years of the Empire.

However later in the Imperial age, as a result of closer ties with various regions of the Empire, there was increased exposure and conversion to different cults and rituals.

From the 3rd century AD these deities were gradually accepted by the state religion. Those who did not find consolation in the official practices could turn to the widespread mystery cults which promised individual redemption and the protection from evil. During the Empire, even more than the Eleusinian mysteries, already widely diffused in classical Greece, the Egyptian devotion to Isis, and the Phrygian Great Mother (Cybele) gained hold.

Cybele was identified with the goddess of the harvest, Ceres, while Mithras, derived from the Iranian sun god, gained the popular veneration of soldiers.

Wall painting of the god Mithras, a sun god of Iranian origin. The Mithraeum, Marino.

The Iseum at Pompeii

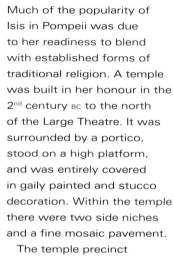

Much of the popularity of Isis in Pompeii was due to her readiness to blend with established forms of traditional religion. A temple was built in her honour in the 2nd century BC to the north of the Large Theatre. It was surrounded by a portico, stood on a high platform, and was entirely covered in gaily painted and stucco decoration. Within the temple there were two side niches and a fine mosaic pavement.

The temple precinct also included a number of other altars; a *purgatorium*, containing a tank thought to have contained holy water from the Nile; and a large room for reunions and possibly initiation ceremonies.

When these buildings were discovered in the mid-18th century many of the paintings, temple vessels and fittings were still intact.

They have sadly disappeared but the graffiti left by visitors at the time bears witness to the admiration they then aroused. A statue of Isis in the archaic style, holding a metal rattle (*sistrum*) in her right hand and the symbol of life (*ankh*) in the left, was found in a corner of the portico.

There were daily rituals celebrated by priests and priestesses within the precinct. Before dawn the image of the goddess was shown to worshippers gathered in front of the temple who greeted her by shaking the *sistrum*.

Prayers and contemplation lasted until dawn and were followed by an invocation to the birth of a new day.

Another ritual took place in the afternoon, devoted to adoration of the holy water. On certain days of the year she was the focus of sumptuous celebrations, the most important of which was the *navigium Isidis* on 5 March.

This was a feast to celebrate the opening of the navigation season after the winter when Isis was venerated as the

Statue of
Isis, from the
temple of Isis
in Pompeii.
National
Archaeological
Museum,
Naples.

patron of sailors and seafarers.

Between the end of
October and the beginning of
November *Isia*, was celebrated.
This was a commemoration
of the discovery of the body

of Osiris (killed and cut into
pieces by his brother Seth)
by his sister Isis who put
him together again and,
through her magical powers,
brought him back to life.

Statue of
Isis, from the
temple of Isis
in Pompeii.
National
Archaeological
Museum,
Naples.

THE SITE TODAY

Wall painting,
1st century AD.
Pompeii, House
of the Vettii.
The splendid
decoration of
the houses in
Pompeii are a
continual source
of fascination
and bear
witness to the
past glory of the
city.

To visit Pompeii today is to come very close to time travel. We can easily imagine the life led by its inhabitants, by those rich Romans who decided to leave the capital to live in the more attractive and peaceful region of the splendid Bay of Naples. The city below Vesuvius, with its buildings, objects, decorations and monuments, brings back the daily life of its inhabitants most vividly. Beyond the city, in the villas at Boscoreale or ancient Oplontis, we can appreciate the atmosphere of seclusion in the remains of buildings that were both luxurious retreats and flourishing agricultural businesses.

In 1980, a few days before an earthquake seriously damaged a number of houses in Pompeii, the whole area had fortunately been photographed, forming a collection of some 18,000 images. Generous financial support, if not sufficient for a total restoration, sponsored a team of experts to consolidate the walls employing materials used in antiquity, such as wood, plaster and bricks, instead of the reinforced concrete which had caused irreparable damage.

Various solutions were adopted for roofing the buildings. Where enough of the original structure survived the roof was faithfully recreated in similar materials.

If the remaining walls did not provide sufficient evidence as to the nature of the original roof, a 'provisional' solution was adopted which did not make direct contact with the ruins. When no trace of the original roof survived an 'umbrella' solution was chosen to protect the area from further deterioration.

House of Loreius Tiburtinus, after restoration, detail of the small fountain and wall painting. 1st century AD. Pompeii.

THE NATIONAL ARCHAEOLOGICAL MUSEUM IN NAPLES

Group of statues of women from the Villa of the Papyrus, Herculaneum, now in the National Archaeological Museum, Naples. The figures used to be referred to as the Danaides.

Nearly all of the most precious objects and works of art from the cities buried by Vesuvius are in the National Archaeological Museum in Naples. These collections date from the time of the Bourbons, heirs to the Farnese, who brought from Rome many works of art such as the *Hercules*, the *Farnese*

Bull and the *Tyrannicides*.

Whole rooms are devoted to the sculpture from the Villa of the Papyrus in Herculaneum, including the celebrated bronze statues, initially thought to be dancers and later associated with the myth of the Danaides, the daughters of Danaus, condemned for eternity to pour water into a well for having murdered their husbands on their wedding night.

A whole wing of the museum houses wall paintings from the two sites, with the Four Styles of Pompeii well represented: these encompass mythological subjects, landscapes, fantastical architecture and still life.

Exhibitions on Pompeii

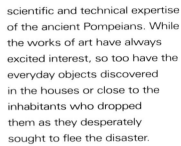

Garden with stone heads of Hermes and a fountain, wall painting from the House of the Golden Bracelet, Pompeii. Many of the wall paintings from Pompeii have become well-known through exhibitions.

There have been many exhibitions devoted to the extraordinary riches recovered from the cities buried by Vesuvius. Some have concentrated on the wall paintings from Pompeii and from Stabia, others on the gold from Oplontis while others still have focused on the erotic paintings, or on the natural, scientific and technical expertise of the ancient Pompeians. While the works of art have always excited interest, so too have the everyday objects discovered in the houses or close to the inhabitants who dropped them as they desperately sought to flee the disaster.

Multimedia resources were used for the first time in the big exhibition *Rediscovering Pompeii*, which took place in Rome in 1993. This included computer-generated three-dimensional reconstructions of the buildings and studies of the roots, seeds and pollen from the fossilized plants.

In recent years interest has not declined and visitors have continued to crowd exhibitions in Italy and elsewhere, such as the travelling *History of an eruption: Pompeii, Herculaneum, Oplontis* which after a period in Naples and Brussels opened in 2004 in Trieste.

THE AREA SURROUNDING POMPEII

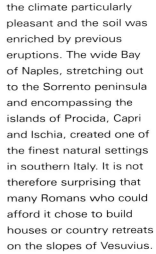

View of the island of Capri, in the Bay of Naples.

Pompeii and the surrounding area, just south of Naples, was even in Roman times particularly densely populated. Proximity to the sea made the climate particularly pleasant and the soil was enriched by previous eruptions. The wide Bay of Naples, stretching out to the Sorrento peninsula and encompassing the islands of Procida, Capri and Ischia, created one of the finest natural settings in southern Italy. It is not therefore surprising that many Romans who could afford it chose to build houses or country retreats on the slopes of Vesuvius.

The site of Herculaneum with its fine houses and well-ordered streets, between the slopes of Vesuvius and the sea, was perhaps even more attractive than Pompeii.

HERCULANEUM

Herculaneum met the same fate as Pompeii as it too was covered and sealed for centuries by a thick layer of ash following the eruption of August in 79 AD. Another city, Resina, was built roughly covering the site of the buried Roman one. Herculaneum was first discovered by chance at the beginning of the 18th century while excavations for a well were in progress: gradually the Roman city was uncovered. Enormous practical difficulties were posed by the existence of the superimposed modern city.

Now, more than a thousand years after its destruction, Herculaneum has revealed much of its original beauty and charm as a seaside settlement.

One can walk down the neatly ordered street with two main 'decumani' crossed by five 'cardines'. Entering from the third 'cardo', which runs from the avenue closest to the sea, the first two houses are the House of Argus and the House of the hotel, so called because it was thought to have been a guest house in the last period of the city. Looking past the ancient houses one can see the modern city not so very different in the

View of the main street (*decumanus maximus*) in Herculaneum.

Room with mosaic pavement, first half of 1st century AD. Herculaneum, baths. The baths were as richly decorated as any of the grand houses in Pompeii.

View of some
of the houses
excavated at
Herculaneum.

arrangement of the houses
and its panoramic location.

There were baths too in
Herculaneum, an essential
feature in any prosperous
Roman resort for those
seeking refuge from the
city and all the benefits of a
relaxing climate. There was
also a *palaestra*, the wide open
exercise public ground, with a
luxuriously decorated portico
with columns decorated
with stucco and a cruciform
swimming-pool more than
86 metres long, probably for
cold water bathing. A first-
floor loggia overlooking the

exercise ground was the
perfect vantage point to
watch the young athletes
doing their exercises.

Among the houses at
Herculaneum the Samnite
House is a remnant of
the oldest settlement in
Herculaneum: other houses
bear traces of the pre-Roman
community. But Herculaneum
was, like Pompeii founded
by the Oscans, before being
ruled by the Samnites and
then the Etruscans, a pattern
common to the whole region.

Whereas space allowed
for the building of ample

View of a Herculaneum street (*cardo* IV) with a half-timbered house. The houses of the poor were made of wood and bamboo and rose a number of storeys to save space.

Following pages: Highly sophisticated polychrome wall mosaic, showing mythical figures, from the House of Neptune and Amphitrite, Herculaneum.

homes in Pompeii, the site at Herculaneum, squeezed between Vesuvius and the sea, created more problems.

The houses were narrower and more closely built, and even poorer houses rose to more than one level, as in the 'House of the Graticcio', built on a number of levels in wood and bamboo with each storey occupied by a separate family as in a modern apartment block.

The Villas at Boscoreale and Oplontis

North of Pompeii, at Boscoreale two villas were unearthed between 1897 and 1900, although today sadly nothing but scant ruins remain.

Nevertheless these secluded villas overlooking the Bay of Naples complete our picture of life in the Roman period, when richly decorated retreats were built far from urban communities. Some hundred vases and precious silver objects, now in the Louvre, were unearthed at Boscoreale. Paintings from this area can be seen not only in Naples but also in the Metropolitan Museum in New York, or in Paris, Brussels and Amsterdam.

The villa at Oplontis is more intact: systematic excavation began in 1964, although random discoveries had been made on the site in the 19th and 20th centuries. The villa is a splendid complex with paintings and stucco decoration. Oplontis was between Herculaneum and Pompeii, at the level of the present day Torre Annunziata and Torre del Greco. The villa is thought to have belonged to Poppea, Nero's second wife or at least to her family, the *gens poppaea*, on the basis of an inscription on an amphora. Certainly the size of the structure suggests a family of considerable importance.

The grounds included a garden and private baths as well as all the working buildings of a flourishing agricultural concern.

Landscape with a small temple, wall painting from the villa at Boscoreale. National Archaeological Museum, Naples.

Visiting Pompeii Today

The site at Pompeii creates a more vivid impression of life in Roman city than any other excavation. Here are not just the foundations of houses and public buildings, but a whole city spread before us with many of its key buildings preserved. There are not only temples, theatres and baths but also private houses and shops, often with their furniture and equipment, together with taverns and hotels and even a brothel (lupanare) with ten small rooms on two floors covered in erotic paintings and graffiti left by clients. Among the streets and alleys of Pompeii, one has the impression that the inhabitants have only slipped away and might return at any moment, but life was frozen in time forever here by the unexpected and terrible eruption of 24 August 79 AD.

Wall painting
from the
triclinium
Villa of Poppea,
Torre Annunziata
(ancient
Oplontis).